NO
APPOINTMENT
NEEDED

NO APPOINTMENT NEEDED

Case Histories From a Counselor's File

BERNHARD AAEN

Review and Herald
Publishing Association

Washington, D.C.
Nashville, Tennessee

ſʀ

Editor: Bobbie Jane Van Dolson
Book Design: Kaaren Kinzer
Cover: Alan Forquer and Kaaren Kinzer

2

Library of Congress Cataloging in Publication Data

Aaen, Bernhard, 1918-
  No appointment needed.

  1. Pastoral counseling—Case studies. 2. Aaen,
Bernhard, 1918-   I. Title.
BV4012.2.A15   253.5   80-20249

ISBN 0-8280-0025-5   Printed in U.S.A.

CONTENTS

DEDICATION

Many years ago I heard that before a man's life is complete he must have a son, build a house, and write a book. Having met the first two criteria long since, and having been careless enough to quote this formula to my family, I have been given occasional reminders by my wife, Penny, my sons, Bernie and Victor, and my daughter, Peggy, to sit down and meet the third requirement. So to these loved ones, whose confidence seems unlimited (and I suspect sometimes not too well founded), I gratefully dedicate this small volume.

INTRODUCTION

A four-o'clock appointment with the academic dean was bearing down upon me as I listened to a student describe at length some of the problems that seemed to depress him like the combined weight of all the tragedies since the time of Adam. Glancing at my watch as surreptitiously as possible, I saw four o'clock come and go. As the minutes ticked by, the problems of this young man seemed to be more and more trivial, and the importance of my appointment with the dean upstairs seemed greater and greater. Eventually the boy seemed to exhaust his troubles, and I arose, wished him God's blessing, and hurried to the dean's office.

Apologizing for my ten-minute-late arrival, I explained that there was a boy sitting in the office at four o'clock who seemed to have poor terminal facilities. He needed to tell his troubles to someone, and it just seemed that he could not finish on time. The answer of Dean Schneider revealed a measure of the man. "Let them talk," he said. "Sometimes students' problems can't wait, and I have plenty to do to keep me busy, even if you are a little late to your appointment. Just let them talk."

Thinking back on this experience later that day, I thought of how many times young people had expressed a need to have someone listen to their problems. My mind drifted back through the years to students at Laurelwood Academy, and those in our academy and college in Indonesia; students at the University of the Pacific, where I taught for two years; young people at Southeast Asia Union College in Singapore, and at Pacific Union College.

Through the years as a parent, teacher, school administrator, recruiter, minister, and counselor, it has been my privilege to spend many hours listening to and talking with students, future students, and former students. Occasionally the question of counseling as a career arises, and if I detect a sensitivity, a genuine concern, for others, I encourage that young person to consider a career in counseling. Inevitably, questions arise. "What does a counselor do? What training must he have?"

This book is addressed to people who love people, and who are interested in the dynamics of counseling. Perhaps you will find it helpful and, I hope, interesting. While I have read, at one time or another, as class assignments or by choice, most of the major theories and theorists in the counseling field, I take Jesus as my model. Although the quality of compassion was always present, His method of approach varied from individual to individual, according to the situation and the personality. At the risk of sounding simplistic, let me state that modern counselors are successful when they follow the principles of Christ, and they fail when they depart from those principles. This is the measure I apply to any "authority" who makes claims to success in this rather inexact field.

In Jesus' teaching and counseling, He used parables and illustrations profusely, so if this book seems to be mostly stories, there is good precedent; the lessons are there, implicit if not explicit. In all cases they retell actual experiences, although names and details have been altered to maintain anonymity as far as possible. Of course, memory is not infallible either.

So if you are among the many who have been approached by friends who wish to unburden themselves, and you wonder how to respond, perhaps this book will be of some help. Remember, no two situations are identical—some are difficult or nearly impossible, some are humorous, some simple. If you keep in close touch with the Master Counselor, and point your friends to Him as the ultimate solution, you may satisfy an acute need.

CHAPTER 1

YOU CAN'T WIN THEM ALL

In Luke 18 we read about a rich young man who sought some counsel from Jesus. He was not only rich, he was a good man— good in that he didn't kick crutches from under cripples, respected his parents, carried on no extra-marital affairs, and had a clear conscience. Or did he?

By his own statement he was blameless. Nevertheless, he felt impelled to ask Jesus if there was not something more he needed to do in order to inherit eternal life, so we can assume he had a small measure of uncertainty about his state of perfection.

Let me digress a moment to notice that this rich ruler opened his interview by flattering the Saviour—"Good Master." Jesus was never diverted by flattery. In this situation, He flatly rejected the compliment; in the case of Nicodemus, He merely ignored it as though He had not heard it. In all cases the Great Counselor turned the focus to the counselee. And that is where the emphasis must be. When the counselor becomes the giver of advice, he's in trouble; when he remains the expositor of God's way, he's safe.

One principle emerges loud and clear from an examination of Jesus' counseling encounters—He had no one formula to apply to all situations. Each case was treated differently, depending on the attitude and the needs of the counselee. This rich ruler was too satisfied with his own perfection. He was sophisticated. He readily agreed with the generally accepted concept that possession of wealth indicated God's blessing and favor. In his thinking, poverty or sickness must mean sin within. This misconcept Jesus decided to hit hard, and He got right to the core of the man's problem—selfishness. It was no tactic for winning the support of the wealthy; but Jesus was not in a popularity contest.

Occasionally a person much like this young ruler claims to want counsel. In reality he or she wants only approval. Take my friend Marty, for instance. Her social life had not been too great; in fact, she had a knack for getting involved with disappointing men. Although she was attractive, smart, and well groomed, the *right* kind of fellows just were not standing in line. Her experiences with the other kind were not the stuff of which happy memories and self-esteem are built.

At the end of one summer she came to my office, and when I asked how her vacation had gone, she announced that while attending summer classes at the university she had finally met a real gentleman, someone who treated her as a lady. No need to be defensive with this man; he wasn't "all hands," as the men she'd dated here at the college were, et cetera, et cetera.

When the rhapsody had subsided, I remarked, "You're really high on this man, aren't you, Marty? Are you going steady with him?"

"Oh, yes. He says I'm the kind of girl he has been looking for. We can talk for hours without his thinking he has to make out all the time."

Later I asked about his religious attitudes.

"Well, he was raised a Catholic, but doesn't consider himself to be one at this time. I'm going to make an Adventist of him. He's such a fine person; he respects my religion."

"Marty, the Good Book says that if the watchman on the wall sees danger and does not warn the city, he will be held responsible. You have come to talk with me about a matter in which you are hardly objective, and although I would like to share your excitement and happiness, I must sound a warning, whether you like it or not. If you want 'a home where the shadows are never lifted,' marry someone outside your own faith. That is not just my personal prejudice, it is a statistically established principle. Many Catholics are good and sincere people, but they are not quick to give up their church allegiance."

"Don't be so worried. This man respects my beliefs, and he treats me like a lady. I used to think as you do, but now I see things differently. If I want him to join my church, he will; he said so. However, I won't ask him to become an Adventist just to marry me. I want him to join because he chooses to. So I won't push him."

"But you will marry him, I take it?"

"Yes. He's the kind of man you don't meet often. He's romantic and refined, and I am sure we will be happy."

She went her way, and I felt sad. Not all counseling situations end happily. Referring again to Luke 18, I read that the young man went away sorrowful, because his wealth stood between him and doing what he should. He asked for counsel, and when the Lord pointed out his duty, he was unwilling to accept. Marty wanted my approval, and was definitely unhappy when I pointed out the hazards she was facing.

The wedding was in neither a Catholic church nor an Adventist church, but sort of on neutral ground—a large church of another denomination. Marty's solution to the difference-of-religion problem was to quit attending her own church. While that sounds logical (he dropped his church affiliation, so she dropped hers), it really did not solve the problem. Without asking permission, her mother-in-law took each of Marty's two daughters for baptism in the Catholic church soon after they were born.

From time to time I would get word from Marty, but the beautiful happiness she sought seemed elusive. Her hero failed in a couple business ventures, and two or three times Marty came home to Mother and Daddy with her little girls. Eventually there was a divorce, and she neither asked for nor received child support. Being a capable woman, she holds a responsible position.

And what about her hero? Rumor has it that he seems to prefer the company of men and lives with a male friend, who was the immediate cause of the divorce.

I meet Marty once or twice a year, but she has never felt impelled to discuss her problems, and lest I seem to come across with "I told you so," I do not ask any questions.

Like Jesus, counselors will inevitably encounter those who do not accept counsel. There will be disappointments. In the case of the rich young ruler, not only was the counselee sorrowful, so was Jesus.

CHAPTER 2

THE RELUCTANT COUNSELEE

As Jesus walked openly through the roads and streets, preaching and performing miracles of healing, He was highly visible, easily accessible to those who sought help. The twentieth-century counselor, lacking His charisma and working in a much more sophisticated and structured environment, may wonder how to get started in his profession.

One chapter in a textbook on counseling is entitled "How Do You Get Them to Come In?" It discusses various ways that a professional counselor can use to get clients—suggesting that he cultivate teachers, pastors, employers, school administrators, or anyone who might be in a position to refer people to him.

Once there was a group of secondary school teachers at an institute. The counselors' section was chaired by a young man with a brand-new M.A. in the field, who asked each person present to introduce himself and describe his work—whether full-time or part-time counseling, and what other responsibilities he might have. One by one those in attendance presented their credentials orally.

One of those present was a motherly woman, who explained that she was not really a trained counselor—in fact, she operated the academy laundry—but since the students came to her so often for help, her principal thought she might profit from listening to the discussions.

After each person had introduced himself, the chairman said, "As our schools become more professional and our staff better trained, we need to educate the students to utilize the expertise available to them. For instance, why on earth should a kid seek counsel from the laundry supervisor? We have to train them to come to the professionals. This means insisting on proper offices, well-identified with a visible sign, attractively furnished, and decorated in good taste. It means discreetly placed announcements in print and in faculty meetings. One good method is simply scheduling the students for appointments and having the principal or deans see to it that they meet those appointments."

Along the path to that M.A., someone should have informed this brash young professional that the qualifications for counseling are caught rather than taught. First of all, there is in the effective counselor an exquisite sensitivity to the feelings of others, a lack of which was demonstrated by this man, who seemed totally unaware that he had needlessly hurt a kind and perceptive woman, one who was all too aware of her lack of a college degree. Sensitivity and caring are the first requisites for anyone who would counsel. Unfortunately, such traits are not conferred with a degree; they may be enhanced by proper teachers, but are really a priceless gift from above. Christ was our example in this, as in all other worthwhile pursuits.

Consider one of the most beautiful counseling episodes in Jesus' life. The woman caught in adultery was probably the most reluctant counselee on record. Tradition says that the Pharisees framed her so they could use her to trap Jesus. The Lord must have despised their willingness to sacrifice her as a pawn in their game.

In his most self-righteous manner, the spokesman said, "Master, this woman was caught in the very act of adultery, and according to Moses, she must be stoned. But what do *You* say?"

They thought surely they had Him. If He agreed with Moses, they would have quickly executed her and reported Him to the Roman authorities for preempting government prerogatives. On the other hand, if He said they should not execute her, He would be denying the revered Mosaic law, and could be expelled from the Temple and discredited. They knew His compassion, and what a difficult decision He would face. The miserable woman also knew that her life was in His hands.

The accusers knew more of the circumstances than they cared to admit. First of all, it takes two to commit adultery. Where was the man? Was he not equally guilty? Further, the same law that decreed stoning for the guilty stated that the accusation was to be made by the wronged husband, and that the witness or witnesses were to cast the first stones.

Instead of replying directly to the loaded question, Jesus chose to deal with the problem in His own way. *The Desire of Ages* says He simply leaned down and wrote in the dust the sins of her accusers. Before reading what He was writing, the men continued to press Him for an answer. Was He going to support Moses, or not? Now standing erect, He said, "He that is without sin among you, let him cast the first stone." It must have been at this point that they became aware of what He had written, for the record says that when He began writing again, they were

16

convicted in their conscience, and, beginning with the eldest, they remembered urgent appointments elsewhere.

I've always wondered if their names were attached to their sins; otherwise, why would they have departed in that exact order? Few of us could bear to see our sins written on the floor of the lobby of the church, for all the worshipers to see. It makes no difference just what He wrote; the fact is that they did not linger to read further. Incidentally, I know of no other record of the Saviour's writing anything during His earthly ministry.

This trapped woman must have found those words in the dust to be the most interesting she had ever read. She and her Lord were probably the only ones to read the whole message, since the audience had all made for the exits, unless the disciples or interested bystanders took the opportunity to see what the Pharisees found so embarrassing.

The record says that when all had left, Jesus looked at her and asked, "Where are your accusers? Isn't anyone going to throw that first rock?"

And with all the gratitude and relief of a condemned criminal whose execution was stayed at the last minute, she answered, "No man is pressing charges, my Lord."

"Well, then, neither do I. Just go, and sin no more."

Let's look at this strange "counseling session" for a moment. As I said before, this poor sinner had no desire to meet the Sinless One. All she knew was that He was a good man who worked miracles. That was common knowledge, so we can assume she felt some awe for Him. How many yearn for someone to talk to, but expect, at least figuratively, to have rocks thrown at them. So they either don't come at all or have to be dragged or pushed to the counselor. One thing is sure, they don't need condemnation. Either they become so defensive that it is useless to point out their mistakes or they are so guilt-ridden that they don't need any more turns of the screw. So then, what does the counselor do? If he must not accuse, should he say, "Well, don't feel so bad, everyone does it. Just don't worry—and quit condemning yourself"?

In other words, should he make them feel comfortable in their sins? No way! Such counselors stop reading at the point where Jesus said, "Neither do I condemn you." The key is in the last statement: "Go, and *sin no more.*"

The woman undoubtedly knew the seventh commandment from childhood. No one needed to point out to her what sin was, and Jesus, who was ever sensitive to human feelings, saw no need for scolding. But He gave her sound admonition, which spoke it all. In essence He was telling her, "Change your ways. You have been spared, but just see that you don't repeat this sin, for you know it *is* sin."

It is not the function of the counselor to pronounce judgment. The counselee has already admitted he goofed and that he has a problem; that's why he's there. Occasionally the counselor needs to help his friend across the desk to see himself more clearly, but that must be done gently and lovingly.

So, when the client recognizes his problem, if the counselor does not pass judgment, what *is* his function? It is simply to lead the sinner to the Source of all peace, the Forgiver of sins and the Reliever of burdens. And that is often difficult. When a student (or older person, for that matter) condemns himself till he can neither sleep at night nor hold his head up in daylight, he must be led to see that Jesus casts forgiven sins behind His back and treats the sinner as if he had never sinned. Beautiful!

A coed came to me, worried that the theology major she was dating seemed to be falling in love with her.

"What's so bad about that?" I asked. "He's a fine fellow, and you'd make a great minister's wife."

"That's what *you* think. I've had an *abortion*."

"OK. You've sinned. How do you know what *his* past is? Anyway, do you believe God has forgiven you?"

"Oh, yes, long ago. But . . ."

"But what? If He forgave you, don't you have a right to expect others to forgive you as well? And should you not forgive yourself? And if you're forgiven, aren't you just as worthy as any other girl?"

"Then suppose he asks me to marry him. Am I to say, 'Oh, by the way, there's a little episode in my diary you might be interested in.' That seems like a dirty trick, doesn't it?"

"Well, remember, you don't know *his* past. He may not have been involved overtly in the same behavior as you were, but doubtless there *are* chapters in his diary that he's not proud of either. Society has scaled certain sins as more scarlet than others, but the Lord gave us no such yardstick. And besides, where do you read in the Good Book that you must wear a placard itemizing your past indiscretions for the protection of the unsuspecting public? Thank God, our past is past as long as it's confessed. Don't worry about your young theologian; he's playing a game called 'finding a wife,' and there are all manner of risks, but if he places the whole scenario in his Saviour's hands, he'll come out all right. The Lord might think you're just right for this boy. Just mark this statement: Purity is a condition of the mind as well as the body. The Lord despises dirty-minded-ness, in virgins as well as nonvirgins. That goes for both sexes."

Another girl came to me voluntarily—no one dragged her, for the simple reason that she had not visibly violated the accepted norms. Nevertheless, she sat there twisting her handkerchief as though she were wringing the neck of Satan himself. What was the problem?

"Well, you see, I have this boyfriend who has always behaved himself, and there have been no big temptations. Until last night. Elder Aaen, I'm ashamed to say this, but we went too far. And I didn't even resist."

Somehow this girl didn't seem the type. But then we're all human, and I registered no shock. Thinking she might have more to say, I asked her whether they had left campus. Oh, yes, they had gone to a concert in San Francisco.

"Did you go in his car?"

"No, he doesn't have a car. We rode with one of the faculty members."

"How was the concert?"

"Oh, fine. The problem was on the way home."

At this, I became puzzled, and plunged ahead with questions, and was later glad that I had.

"Did you come home with the teacher?"

"Oh, yes, of course. I wouldn't break my agree-ment with the dean. We stopped for a bite to eat, but stayed with the group."

"Pardon me, but I'm mystified. When did this problem take place, if you were chaperoned all the way?"

"It was in the car. We *held hands* all the way home!"

And the sobs left no doubt as to her remorse.

If beauty is in the eye of the beholder, guilt *can* be in the mind of the guilty one. My immediate reaction was to view it as a big joke, and I had to choke back gales of relieved laughter. But it was no joke to the suffering girl. Watching her agonize, I felt she would gladly have amputated the hand that offended. So we treated her problem seriously, though I did try to reduce her anxiety by putting her relatively innocuous lapse into perspective. I assured her that holding hands was probably not in the category of lust, and that it was not proscribed in the Bible.

So let's say there are at least three reactions that the Saviour avoided in dealing with sensitive sinners—denunciation (scolding), shock, and derision. Any problem that is serious to the counsel-seeker must be treated seriously.

Back to our first concern—how do counselees find a counselor? Nicodemus sought the Lord secretly; he was reluctant to admit that he needed counsel. The rich young ruler came openly, wanting approval. And the woman in John 8 was dragged before Him, expecting the worst. In every case Jesus responded compassionately. Two thousand years later, that is still the key to successful counseling. Some students may seek help privately, in a casual setting. A true follower of the Lord's example will not say, "Please come to me during office hours; I am busy now." Another may come directly to the counselor's desk, professing to want help but unwilling to accept it. The third type may be sent by the dean or the principal, having no choice. May we always have sensitivity and compassion. The textbooks call it "establishing rapport." So be it. Just so they know we care.

CHAPTER 3

KNOW THE AGENDA OR DON'T GO

The girl sat in my office because she had been accepted on scholastic probation, and one condition of admission was a weekly chat with a counselor. As a rather defensive non-Christian, she was explaining her philosophy of life. She came from a broken home, and some distant Adventist relatives had encouraged her to come to our college. Quite obviously she was not going to opt for our church. I listened quietly, sometimes making a comment or asking an occasional leading question.

She mentioned that on a Caribbean cruise she had been initiated into what she called "love." Anticipating my disapproval, she hastened to explain that her mother had prepared her for the big bad world by advising her, "Never do anything you don't feel right about." That's a variation of the theory that if it feels good, do it. Ann Landers and Dear Abby have shot that argument full of holes, repeatedly and deftly and logically. But my young friend apparently hadn't read Ann and Abby on that topic.

I did not feel constrained to push my morality on her at that time, so I let the matter drop, and listened for the rest of our appointed time. The next week when she sat in the office, things had not been going so well with her studies, and she seemed to be in a more thoughtful, less belligerent mood.

"I don't know why I can't buckle down and study sometimes. I get to thinking about myself, and frankly, I hate myself. I'd just like to wipe out everything and start over again."

"Then, you'd live your life differently if you could do it over, right? Would you say there are some guilt areas that bother you?"

"Yes, that's true. I suppose it's common to regret certain things, but I still feel uncomfortable."

"If you had it to do over again, would you take that cruise you told me about last week?"

"Well, no, I wouldn't. My memories of it aren't all that great. It seemed romantic and exciting at the time—I was just 18—but I wish that I hadn't gone or that I had at least used better judgment."

I refrained from reminding her that at the time, her conscience, supported by her mother's shallow dictum, had said everything was just great. It didn't seem to be the time to try to untangle the fallacy by which she had made her decisions—the fallacy that one can trust his impulses for a right decision.

Repeatedly I have tried to emphasize to students the importance of making decisions, setting boundaries, ahead of time. Few people, I am sure, deliberately plan to get into trouble. Rather, they find themselves in situations for which they have made no provision, and then lack courage to resist.

I am reminded of a girl in Singapore who was quite impressed by a young fellow she had been introduced to. Some days after their meeting, he phoned and asked for a date. He would pick her up at her flat that evening about seven. Since it was Saturday night and she had no other plans, and he was handsome, she was excited. But not speechless.

"Where are we going?" she asked.

"Oh, just out."

"Yes, I know, but out where?"

"Oh, I don't know. Maybe get something to eat."

"For the whole evening?"

"Well, I thought we'd drive out to Changi Beach for a while."

"Yes, but what would we do at Changi Beach?"

"Listen, Chick, if you don't know what couples go to Changi Beach on Saturday night for, maybe you had better come along and I'll show you."

"Thanks a lot, Buster, but I'm afraid you just wasted a phone call. Changi Beach on Saturday night, with no agenda, just isn't my cup of tea. Sorry."

When she told me about that encounter, I congratulated her. First of all, she didn't ask herself whether she felt "right" about the guy. Actually she was quite excited about him. But her key word was *agenda*. She just had to know what was on the agenda before she would trust her feelings. No waiting for the crunch to see if her conscience felt good about it. To trust her feelings when under pressure was not for her. I admired her good judgment, and told her so.

"As a matter of fact," she said, "I very much wanted to go out with him. I don't get that many dates, and he was cool. It's no fun sitting at home on Saturday nights. But I decided long ago that I'd never put myself into the position of having to back away from a situation I should not have gotten into in the first place."

It is so easy to pray, "Lead us not into temptation," and then blindly walk into traps that a 10-year-old could see. Why? Simply because we like to trust our consciences or, if you please, our feelings.

How often have I heard girls say, "But Dr. Aaen, I *like* to play with fire." Or "I can handle the situation. I know what I'm doing."

So how about this faculty known as conscience? Can't it be educated to trustworthiness? Surely it *can* be educated, and must be. But to deliberately place the conscience under test is to gamble in a way the Lord never intended us to. The safest driver is not the one who deliberately takes chances, but the one who avoids them except when it is absolutely necessary. I have been a pilot for three decades, and I expect to die in bed, because my instructors have ingrained in me the fact that there are old pilots and bold pilots, but no old bold pilots. Airplanes are unforgiving critters, and so is temptation. One of my students in Java used to say, "Never trouble trouble till trouble troubles you." That well-worn proverb still makes sense.

God gave us five wonderful senses, but He also gave the same to the animals. The difference is that He gave each of us the divine gift of a mind with which to weigh and evaluate and predict. Human beings can relate one situation to another. We can plan ahead, and make decisions when we are sober and deliberate. Then when the heat is on, we can choose to act according to previously settled guidelines.

When I was in the army in India during World War II, I watched soldiers deliberately become intoxicated before going to the prostitutes, simply because they knew they could not proceed when sober. In other words, they deliberately anesthetized their consciences so their feelings could rule rather than their minds. And as far as I could tell, they all felt cheap afterward.

The conscience needs to be educated and then

listened to. But too often we confuse the feelings of the moment with conscience, and wonder later why we feel so bad because of what happened under the stress of strong emotion. Perhaps it is not accurate to equate conscience with feelings, but at least the young people I talk with attest strongly to the conviction that feelings can too easily override conscience. Only later does conscience accuse us, and we face those destructive guilt pangs.

Going back to the girl who went on the Caribbean cruise. Her misguided mother had led her to think that somehow she would know what to do, and that her feelings would be a safe guide. It may be that such counsel would work if decisions were made retroactively. The trouble is that we are forced to make decisions now and ponder them later. So why can't we ponder them *first,* and avoid having to try to think above the clamor of a screaming glandular system, which knows nothing of conscience or the Ten Commandments? Only your God-given brain knows whether you have the approval of your Saviour and your family and fellow Christians.

So, think ahead. Know the agenda or don't go. Seek the Lord's help. One girl recently told me that she finally got up courage to ask her date to pause for a word of prayer (her roommate's suggestion) before leaving the dormitory lobby. She really thought the guy might not even want to take her if she made such a startling suggestion. Anyway, she did, and the fellow said, "Hey, that's neat. First time any girl ever asked me to do that." She said it was one of the most interesting evenings of her life. There was no awkwardness, no lack of things to talk about. Each knew what to expect of the other. Knowing she could trust her date, the girl felt comfortable from the first. There was no sparring, no games, just good fun.

CHAPTER 4

SENSITIVITY MAKES SENSE

Young people often get the twisted idea that making mistakes is good preparation for *not* making mistakes. I suspect it becomes sort of an excuse for sampling forbidden activity.

After several sessions in the office, spent mostly relating her tale of woe, the young woman counselee paused long enough for me to direct her thoughts to the future. What did she think she'd like for a lifework?

"Well, I think that after all I've been through, I should be a counselor. Nobody could throw anything at me that I haven't tried. I've seen it all."

"You feel that your experience in giving in to temptation qualifies you to counsel, right?"

"Sure, don't you think so? I mean, how can a person counsel who hasn't experienced?" Pause. "You look like you don't think I could do it. I know the problems of young people because I've been there."

"By that reasoning, Eve was correct in wanting to know evil as well as good. Satan, who *really* knows evil, must be the greatest counselor of all. And Jesus, the Sinless One, would, of course, be the poorest. No, I don't think your fling with drugs and rebellion qualifies you for a career in counseling."

"Why not?"

"Well, for one thing, a counselor must be concerned with others. You have talked to me three times now, for a half-hour each time, and I don't recall your expressing any solicitude for your roommate, your parents, your brother, or your friends. Your favorite topic is yourself."

Like the rich young ruler of Luke 18, she went away sorrowful. And so was I.

Students often ask about becoming counselors, and in most cases I suspect they think of it as a career of advice-dispensing, of listening to exciting secrets—in short, of being the expert. Not so. Whenever you begin dispensing advice, you run the risk of being held responsible for the outcome—the client feels minimum obligation to make a strong effort at a solution. He can blame you for failure instead of himself.

So, what does a good counselor do? Typically, he tries to gain the confidence of his visitor by showing real concern. Then he encourages the counselee to verbalize the problem, and that's not always easy. Sometimes he must wait patiently while the person tests him on a couple nonthreatening matters first. I recall a time when my neighbor offered to sharpen a friend's scissors. She first brought him an old rusty pair, which he put in good working condition. She tested them, and only when she was sure he was competent did she let him touch her best shears. He teased her about not trusting him, but at the same time he clearly understood the dynamics of her method. Students use the same strategy; they want to know they can trust a counselor on a small matter before trusting him or her with what lies nearest their hearts. Patience is the best virtue at this stage of the relationship.

When the real problem has been spread out on the table, so to speak, the counselor asks his friend to list the possible solutions. Notice that he resists the temptation to donate a share of his impressive wisdom by assigning a course of action that may seem to him to be obvious and perfectly logical. When the counselee has suggested all the alternatives he or she can think of, the counselor may then ask whether this or that possibility has been considered. He is not making a prescription, but rather naming possible courses of action.

This leads into the critical point in the relationship. *The counselee must choose the course of action,* and that quite possibly may not be the one his mentor would have chosen. However, the act of choosing has the great virtue of forcing a degree of commitment from the client.

The next steps are planning, encouragement, and follow-up. The caring that began the relationship will be tested—and proved—by the continued concern of the counselor.

Where does the pastoral, the spiritual, aspect come into the process? That depends on the degree of receptivity of the counselee. I nearly always close with prayer, even if the person professes no inclination to put his problems into the Lord's hands. If, on the other hand, he welcomes divine aid, we may stop and pray at any appropriate point in the discussion. I always have Bibles in several versions within reach, and frequently cite a scriptural illustration, or principle, or solution. Having been an ordained minister for more than twenty-five years, I counsel with a strong Biblical bias, which has so far always been respected.

Back to our "experienced" young woman who thought herself ipso facto a counselor: one could just as logically say that one is a dolphin because he fell overboard, swam awhile, and was fished out of the saltwater.

Actually, when asked what traits are important for the counselor to possess, I list first the one we just discussed, *caring.* Then I mention *confidentiality.* The counselor's ability to help is in direct proportion to the information he is given, and if the clients don't trust him to keep their secrets, they won't talk. Next comes the ability to be *nonjudgmental,* which is closely related to *unshockability.* Jesus recognizes that we are all at different stages in our spiritual and social growth, and He accepts us where we are. By the same token, the counselor must accept counselees where they are and pray and work with them for growth. If and when they want his values, they'll ask. Actually, they doubtless already know where he stands.

Before we proceed, let me point out why most students come to a pastor or a teacher or a friend rather than to a parent, who would seem to be the ideal source of help. I've asked countless young people, "Have you ever discussed this topic with your mother or dad?" Almost invariably the answer is an emphatic, "No, of course not. They'd get all bent out of shape, and yell at me." Or they may feel that the parents would panic, or punish them. If the problem involves sex, they say this is something that is never discussed at home. In most families the lines of communication are just not open for certain topics. If parents communicated properly with their offspring, all counselors could retire.

The last important characteristic for a successful counselor is *humility.* No matter how much one has studied or how high his degree, he will meet problems that baffle, that are not mentioned in the Bible or in case studies. These tend to keep a person humble, but then flattery comes along just often enough to lull the unwary into a false confidence. Remember how Jesus treated Nicodemus' complimentary opening, and how He swept aside the flattering statements (not even a modest Thank you) of the woman at the well. Humility drives the counselor to the only real sources of help—prayer and Bible study. If he lets loose of those two boons, he either begins following one or another of the so-called experts or develops his own favorite approach. The Christlike method of counseling puts the counselor and his narrow formulas into the background, and applies a truly eclectic approach to each situation. As we state elsewhere in this book, Jesus never used the same technique twice, but adapted His approach to the unique circumstances of each case.

CHAPTER 5

SOMETIMES COUNSELING IS FUN

Not all student visits deal with what I consider problems. To the student it may be a problem, but to the counselor it's pure joy. To illustrate:

I sat at my desk at our college in Java, with the door open to the lovely tropical morning. Presently the doorway was darkened by a perplexed young man, whom I invited in. Without preface he sat down and said, "Mr. Aaen, I have a problem."

The statement was familiar, but not from this boy, a senior theology student whose biggest flaw was getting so lost in a book that he occasionally missed an appointment. A real bookworm, and a promising evangelist.

"OK, Willie, what's the problem?"

"You know Thio May Ling? Well, yesterday as I came out of the dining room, she smiled at me!"

"That's a problem?" I blurted out. May Ling was a real charmer. I recalled some three years before when she had breezed into this same office and announced that she'd come to school. At that time one look at her raised a whole array of warning flags—she was painted, bejeweled, and bedecked like a movie star. Plainly she enjoyed my surprise. When reminded that we had no application from her, she had said, "Oh, that's all right; I have plenty of money." I then asked if she was a Christian, to which she replied sweetly, "Of course not. I'm an atheist, and politically I'm a Communist." Obviously she was having fun trying to shock me.

"Well, then, what do you want to come to this school for? We're quite different from you in the way we think and act and dress. And we don't talk politics much, either."

Still the same twinkle in her eye, and the same smile. "Oh, I just thought it would be fun to attend an American school for a change. I've attended only Communist schools so far, and I'd like to see if you really eat people."

"First of all, this isn't an American school. We do have two American families and one Canadian family on the staff, but the rest of the faculty are Indonesians. Our curriculum is Indonesian. English is the medium of instruction in the college courses, but Indonesian is used in middle school. I think you're in the wrong place. Our students don't wear jewelry or makeup and don't drink, smoke, or dance. The Bible is a required course every year, and religious services are an integral part of the regimen. A dress such as you're wearing would not meet our standards."

But May Ling had come 400 miles and wasn't about to be turned away. She filled in the application, never doubting that we'd accept her. Even when the dean of girls condemned her entire wardrobe as immodest, she merely took the dresses to Bandung to her grandparents, and bought suitable ones. After some deliberation, our committee accepted her, albeit with misgivings.

The Bible teachers hardly knew what to do with a student who didn't believe in God and who asked questions they'd never dreamed of. But both she and the school survived the first year, and after fall Week of Prayer of the second year, she joined the baptismal class, mainly because she wanted to know *everything* about our beliefs. May Ling had the priceless quality of acting enthusiastically on whatever she was convinced was right. Her extremely sharp mind made some of the Bible teachers dig for answers to her perplexing but incisive questions.

After the spring Week of Prayer, Elder Mamora assured me that May Ling was truly ready for baptism. As I dipped her into the waters of the stream, I thought how close we had come to denying her application nearly two years earlier. As she rose from the water, the smile on her face was still there, only I thought it had more meaning now. What a transformation, from dedicated Communist to dedicated Christian!

But back to Willie and his "problem."

"I thought you were engaged to one of the nurses at the hospital, Willie."

"Yes, Mr. Aaen, but that was yesterday. Today everything looks different."

I assured the boy that I understood, and that he must think and pray about this new turn of events, and that things would probably work out quite pleasantly. Also, I let him know that May Ling was a fine young woman, and that he should not feel inferior just because her family was well off and he had to work his way. We had prayer, and he floated out of the office on his own airy cloud.

Within the hour my door was darkened again, this time by the ever-smiling May Ling.

"Mr. Aaen, I've got a problem."

"Well, May Ling, I'd say it can't be too big a problem. You look very happy to me."

"You know Willie Lee? Well, yesterday at dinner he smiled at me."

"I wouldn't worry too much about that. Willie is very friendly. I dare say he smiles at everyone." Inwardly I was fighting a chuckle.

"But you don't understand. It was the *way* he smiled. Mr. Aaen, I have no time for this silly nonsense of flirting, but you should have seen that smile. I've known Willie for nearly three years now, and I'm sure he never looked at me that way before. What happened?"

I could only say that there is no rational explanation for such things, and that perhaps she should let nature take its course—within the framework of school rules, of course.

Since Willie was graduating in June and since every mission in the union wanted him, he was quite naturally thinking in terms of marriage. Somehow the nurse dropped out of his life, and whatever magic there was in that dining-room encounter continued its yeasty chemistry, so that by the time school was out, they were making wedding plans. My wife was disappointed, since she wanted May Ling to finish her college home-economics course. Like Solomon, I don't profess to understand "the way of a man with a maid," but if ever love worked its mysterious way, it did with them.

By the end of his first year of internship, Willie, with May Ling by his side, had won more than 100 souls to Christ. Recently, when I received their Christmas card, with a photo of them with their two bright-eyed children, my thoughts went back to that little office in Java, to their almost simultaneous appearance with their mutual "problem."

Further back even than May Ling's first dramatic entry to that office, with its one outside door, there was the meeting (in the same room) of the admissions committee one fall, and the application of one Willie Lee. He had been turned down the previous year because he had a police record and was running with a gang of street toughs, totally beyond the control of his parents. One of the members of the committee—I think it was the dean of boys—observed that the boy must want something better, or he would not apply the second time. It was voted, with some misgivings, to take him on probation, and he was so notified. When he first entered that office, I gave him what I considered some pretty straight talk about what it meant to be accepted on probation. He assured me we would have no trouble from him, and we didn't.

The next fall, after the long vacation, he again stood in my office, happy to be back at school. When asked about the summer, he said, "Let me tell you about my first weekend at home. You know my father is lay pastor of one of the Protestant churches in Macassar. Well, he was a bit upset when I went to church on Sabbath, but I promised I'd go to church on Sunday with him. Since his parishioners knew of my old reputation, he was eager to let them know I had changed, so he introduced me to each of them as his son who was studying for the ministry at a seminary in Java. Several of them suggested that he invite *me* to preach, until it became so embarrassing that he did."

"You didn't accept, did you, Willie?" I gasped, remembering that he had taken but one Bible course.

"Well, what could I do? They insisted."

"But you have just begun to study the Bible—no homiletics or anything like that. What did you talk about?"

"Well, the key texts I remembered best were on

the Sabbath, so I preached a sermon on the Sabbath."

"Did the roof fall in? What did your father say?"

"Actually, he was pretty upset at first, but at the door afterward, the people congratulated him so much on his son that he decided he was proud of me after all. One member hurt him a little, I think, when he asked why they didn't have more sermons from the Bible."

The ways of the Lord are inscrutable. What a privilege it is to be a part in helping such young people with their problems.

CHAPTER 6

TRUST IN THE LORD AND DO BETTER

More often than not, young people's problems are in fact too difficult for human solution, and at such times the counselor appreciates the promises and enablings of his Lord.

Consider the case of Terri. The level in my Kleenex box sank perceptibly each Tuesday at five o'clock, when Terri dropped in for her weekly visit. Self-assurance was not her strong point—and with reason.

"I flunked high school, and finally took the GED tests to prove I had finished. I'm dumb, stupid. I didn't think I was college material, so I pushed hamburgers in a fast-food place for two years. That was enough of *that*, so I decided, foolishly, to give college a try. Now that I'm here, I realize that for sure I'm not college caliber. I stare at the pages and can't tell what they say. Because of my crummy high school GPA, I can't get grants or scholarships, and with the basketful of F's I'm headed for, I won't be able to get another loan. I work for my room and board, but even if I could raise tuition money, it would be a waste; I'd just fail again."

Looking at her ACT scores, I saw that there was solid basis for her gloom—not one of the five was above the tenth percentile, meaning that 90 percent or more of the high school seniors, nationwide, who took the tests were above her. I was inclined to agree that she was not "college material"—whatever that may be. I never did really know the essential qualifications for success in college, even when I was admissions officer, with the responsibility for screening applicants. More than twenty years of dealing with college freshmen has failed to convince me that I can predict success or failure with more than a modest batting average.

Nevertheless, here sat Terri, weeping at her dismal scholastic past, her self-image all bent out of shape, and as terrified of a future in the fast-food business as would be any newly condemned galley slave. And, I must confess, I shed a few tears with her, for by her own admission she could not read, and the test scores underlined that deficiency. How *could* she make it in college if she could not comprehend and recall what she read? In college that's the whole game. How could I help this panic-stricken misfit?

Panic-stricken? Could that be the key? Suddenly I remembered that just a year before, Flo was admitted, also on probation because of a ghastly GPA in high school. She came to us from a mental hospital, from which the Lord had rescued her by means of some Morris Venden cassettes. She had enrolled in theology—Greek and all. I had limited her total hours in view of the scholastic demands made on aspiring theologians.

About a month after school started, Flo came to my office with real worry on her pretty brow. Her conversion had made her such a radiant Christian that I was surprised at the change, and said so.

"I'll tell you what worries me. It's a big exam in Intro to Theology. A hundred points, just like that.

And I never do well under pressure. I've always blown the big tests."

"OK, Flo, let me ask you a couple questions. Do you think the Lord brought you here?"

"Of couse. That's one thing I *do* know for sure."

"And do you think He's going to let you down now?"

"Well, I suppose not. No, He surely won't."

"And, Flo, have you studied regularly?"

"Yes, I have. I haven't dared miss a lesson. Since I did so badly in high school, I don't dare skip a class or an assignment. I'm really not a good student—never have been—so I have to dig. I know it."

"OK, then you just tell the Lord you're claiming James 1:5. And *don't worry* about the test result. You've done your best, and if the Lord wants you to get a C, B, or A, the result will be His, not yours. Don't sweat about the grade, just do what you can, and see what He may have for you. Worry creates panic, which can congeal the thinking processes as a deepfreeze does molasses. And further, how can God answer your request for a clear mind if you really don't believe Him?"

We had prayer together and she left, promising to accept any grade the Lord sent.

Some days later she met my wife and me on the campus, her smile radiating good news like a stadium floodlight.

"You'll never believe this! I walked into that test without a care in the world, determined not even to think about scores or percentages. I answered each question as well as possible and left, completely placid and unruffled. I didn't even call Dr. Veltman's office to find out how I did. And you know—when the papers were returned, I got 100 out of 100. Best I've ever done in my life. Praise the Lord."

And we did praise the Lord. Flo followed the same formula in her other studies, and while she hasn't maintained a 4.0 GPA, she has never fallen below 3.0, which is a B. And she tackles any subject with confidence—not in herself, but in her Lord.

All this came to mind as I dried my tears and pondered what I could say to my miserable friend Terri, whose future—scholastically and professionally—seemed so hopeless.

"Terri, do you pray?"

"Oh, yes, Dr. Aaen, I pray every time I open a book or take a quiz. But it doesn't do a bit of good. If God didn't give me the brains when I was born, I guess He isn't suddenly going to make up the deficiency now. My trouble is that I find it hard to accept that He made me stupid. Did He really create some people to spend their lives pushing fast foods for minimum wage?"

Sensing panic as the real grade-point gremlin, I made a suggestion.

"Terri, I'll agree your prospects aren't good. Unless something changes radically, you'll wash out. Now, in view of that, are you willing to try an experiment?"

"Dr. Aaen, I'll try anything. I don't want to be a drudge all my life. But if I'm stupid, I'm stupid, right? What's the experiment?"

"OK. You get up a half-hour early tomorrow morning. Open your Bible to something inspirational—Psalms or the New Testament—and read till you find something that seems just for you. That may take five minutes or the whole half-hour. Then say, 'Lord, this is *Your* day. Everything I do will be to please You, not me. I'm not going to worry about grades or quizzes or tomorrow. I'll just do what needs doing. And since everything is in Your hands,

You decide whether or not I should stay in college. I won't fuss if You want me somewhere else. The grades will be the basis for that decision.' Then at the end of the day you thank Him for His leading, even if you can't see where you're being led.

"Do that each day. Don't worry about how well you're doing in studies or quizzes or tests. Remember that He may have something for you other than college, and if so, He'll tell you. You're just waiting for His direction."

The tears subsided, we had prayer, and she agreed to give it a try, quite sure the Lord would speak through the inevitable and predictable dismissal letter. And I'll admit that I was no oasis of optimism either.

The following week she was right on time. I didn't know whether to dread or hope, but as I opened the door Terri pranced in, flooding my office with joy and cheer.

"Dr. Aaen, you won't believe this! I've had three midterms this week, and got three C's in them. And I haven't worried in the least, before, during, or after! You know something? All my prayers used to be desperate, panicky shouts for help. No more! I just relax and do what I can, and let Him do the worrying."

It sounded almost too simple, too sudden, too perfect. But she had the test results to confirm her optimism, and who was I to place limits on God's ability to answer prayer? We thanked God, and Terri went on her way rejoicing.

When she didn't meet our next appointment, I was worried, so I phoned her, only to hear a cheery voice say she had been so busy with studies that she had forgotten to come in. "Really, Dr. Aaen, I just don't think I need the counseling anymore. The

Lord is my counselor, and things are going just fine. Thanks for the help. I'll call if any further problems come up."

I guess every counselor is trying to work himself out of a job, just as is every doctor—or pastor, for that matter. But few counselor-counselee relationships end quite as abruptly—and happily—as did mine with Terri.

At the end of each quarter I get a computer printout of all student grades, and when this one came, the first name I looked up was Terri's, and there it was, a 2.68 GPA, with no F's or D's or W's. While many students would hope to do better than that, for Terri it was a beautiful testimony of God's willingness to help.

She stopped in to talk over her plans shortly after the second quarter began, saying, "Using the same method—complete trust in God, regular study, and no anxiety—I plan to build my GPA for the next two quarters, and this summer I'll take Anatomy and Physiology so I can apply for nurse's training."

My first impulse was to warn her against overoptimism, but I caught myself. Where was my faith? I remembered J. B. Phillips' book *Your God Is Too Small* and wondered whether *my* God was too small. So I joined Terri in another prayer of thanksgiving and commitment.

CHAPTER 7

LIKE MOTHER, LIKE DAUGHTER?

Every counselor meets a Terri once in a while, and thanks God for the encouragement. But now and then he sees values crumble and erode, and must take comfort in recalling that the Wonderful Counselor Himself did not win all encounters.

I was studying one day in my little office at the academy where I taught. In one corner, at her own small desk, sat my reader, Eunice, correcting papers. Quiet and demure, she was, as usual, minding her own business and working with quiet efficiency. Perhaps no girl ever came to that school from a more sheltered background than she. The comfortable silence was broken by a knock at the door, and in bounced a breezy young girl named Jane. Jane wanted to talk, and as we discussed various matters, I saw no need to ask Eunice to leave the room. As a matter of fact, I had no outer office, and she had her work to do. So Jane talked.

Eventually the conversation got around to what could be called Topic A—the future home. Suddenly Jane's light voice became serious, her eyes dropped, and she said, with a great deal of determination, "I'm going to have a different kind of a home than Mother did." Sensing that here was a girl who belonged to that great army of young people whose family life was less than ideal, I said, "Apparently you think that you can improve upon the kind of home that you came from." With this, Jane looked up, and her eyes began to fill with tears as she said, "You've no idea of the kind of home I came from." And I agreed that I knew nothing of her background. She appeared to be a sweet, innocent Christian girl, and, while I didn't know her well, I had no reason to suspect anything but a normal family situation behind her.

As she talked, I was appalled to learn that her mother had been married six times, five of them since she had divorced Jane's father. These men were anything but pleasant types, and naming over her five stepfathers on her fingers as one would count off birthdays, Jane came to number six. Her voice became bitter as she said, "I hate Jerry." Quickly I pointed out that we should not hate anyone, and said, "Why would you want to hate Jerry?"

At this she became almost hysterical as she poured out all the unkind things that Jerry had said about her own father. Forgetting where she was and who she was, she began to quote the profanity that this crude man had used as he criticized her dad. Before I could stop her, she had spewed out a stream of oaths that would have scorched the ears of a longshoreman. I glanced at Eunice, the sweet and demure one, sitting there trying to grade papers. Her face was red and even her ears were red. Probably no such assault had ever been made upon her sensibilities.

In the course of subsequent counseling sessions with Jane, we discussed at length the elements that make up a successful Christian home. Over and over again she expressed her determination to have but one marriage, and that one the ideal. In due time she graduated, and soon after, I left that campus and didn't see her for some fifteen years. When I encountered her again at camp meeting, I told her that I lived in Angwin. Her face brightened up and she said, "Oh, that's where my children are." Since I had just met her husband, I asked, quite naturally, why the children were in Angwin. As if a faucet had been turned on, the tears began to roll, and Jane said, "Mr. Aaen, I lost custody of my children. This is my second husband."

Seeing no reason to thrust my clumsy fingers among the heartstrings of this sensitive and suffering person, I skipped the obvious questions and merely attempted to talk courage to her as she sobbed there in public. Then while my wife consoled and calmed Jane, her husband explained that she condemned herself severely for having lost custody of her children. I have no way of knowing what happened to that girl in those fifteen years, but my heart aches for her—with all her beautiful dreams of having the ideal home, of not repeating the mistakes of her mother, of being the ideal wife and mother. Obviously she had committed some grave indiscretion, or the court would not have taken her children from her. My heart goes out to those who face grave trials such as these, and I could only feel sympathy for this person so torn by self-incrimination. Musing to myself, I could but think of the text that says the sins of the fathers shall be visited upon the children.

CHAPTER 8

SOME SHIPS SAIL EAST, SOME WEST . . .

The values of girls like Jane, no matter to what stresses they may later be subjected, are beautiful. Between priceless idealism and Satan's sophistication the counselor must tread carefully, lest he destroy the one or encourage the other.

While studying in the graduate school at a large university, I was employed in the teaching of two sections of freshman English. This university was established and governed by a popular Protestant church. One of the students who took my class was Gloria, the daughter of a pastor of a church of that denomination. Winner of a church scholarship, she had traveled across three States, expecting to find at the university those who shared her idealism, her love for the Saviour, and her dreams of Christian service. After about a month of school she came for some counsel in regard to a theme that she had written, and we fell to talking.

It soon became apparent that her idealism was suffering from severe shock as she looked around her and found no one interested in the gospel to all the world or in the sacrifice of the Jesus who was so real to her. She explained that her religion teacher had assured her that the Old Testament was an interesting book of stories, but that she must not take it too seriously. One statement stands out clearly in my memory. She said, "I came here on a scholarship from my church. I came here to develop myself as a Christian soul winner, and no one wants to talk about Jesus. The only person on the campus who seems to share my love of the Lord is a Seventh-day Adventist English teacher." I thanked her for the compliment, and my heart wept with hers at the worldliness all around us, the drinking, the smoking, and the immorality in the dormitories and on the campus, the atheism, the cynicism, and the sophistication that was so disillusioning to this sweet Christian girl.

Many times she visited my little office, and many times we had prayer, and always my burden was the same, that this girl should never lose her idealism in a wicked world. Gloria was studying speech therapy because she felt a burden to help those less fortunate than she was. After two years she moved on to the State university, and when I saw her last, she was still determined to be a speech therapist, but her dresses and makeup all testified that something had been lost—something of the sweetness, something of the simplicity, something of the innocence. Surely someone, perhaps many, will have to answer for the changes in Gloria.

Betsy was another young woman who came into my office at the university for counsel. She was not the most attractive girl, and yet she was a lovable type. Her parents were in the East, and her mother apparently was a very refined and devoted Christian woman. Her father was in the military service and apparently had a different set of standards. He had permitted the girl to smoke, against her mother's wishes. When she came to the university, she wanted desperately to be sophisticated, to be popular, to live as she had been taught by the movies and television that a college girl should live. My efforts to explain to her that these standards, or lack of standards, brought no one any happiness were futile, because she had her mind all made up. "I admire the girl in the room next to me. She can smoke with a great deal more sophistication than I. I still feel uncomfortable, someway, because I feel like my mother is looking over my shoulder and disapproving. This girl can drink almost a limitless number of highballs in an evening and be unaffected by it, and I get giddy if I take more than one. She doesn't care what people think of her. She does what she wants to, when she wants to do it. She can discuss her weekends with the fellows without any embarrassment, and I blush even when she talks. Why can't I be as free as she is?"

Nothing that I said seemed to have much influence upon this star-struck, deluded young modern. Obviously she was not going to be happy in either the world that her mother wanted her to live in or the fantasy world that she thought she wanted to occupy. I took courage in the hope that disillusionment might at some future date cause Betsy to see the wisdom of her mother's way.

Now, several years later, as I think of those two years at the university, I recall Gloria in her innocence, battling worldly influences, and Betsy wishing she were free of a nagging conscience. Where are they now? Was I a positive force in their lives?

CHAPTER 9

THE CASE OF THE MYSTERIOUS HEADACHES

Although the Glorias and Betsys may add gray hair to a counselor, now and then the Lord sends along a reminder that we should not take ourselves too seriously. We'll call this one "The Case of the Lost Headache."

Although she tested well on ACT, her high school GPA dictated that she be on academic probation, so she appeared in my office the first week of school. A 34-year-old survivor of two matrimonial disasters, with two small sons, she was hardly typical of my usually hopeful, bewildered, and rather naive freshman counselees. In fact, she fairly bristled with determination to sculpt a career for herself and ensure support for the kids, independent of the men in her life—past, present, or future. I foresaw no scholastic difficulties, but assigned her a weekly time slot in case she might need encouragement.

At her second appointment she explained a bit more of her circumstances. "I've bought a good used car, since my apartment is too far from the elementary school for the kids to walk, and I'm saving my own energy for tennis class."

In fact, her counseling appointment was immediately after tennis, and she came directly to my office without changing from an expensively brief tennis costume. Should I warn the woman that she might catch cold, or give her a short lecture on appropriate attire? As she waltzed away, presumably home to change, I mentioned my slight discomfiture to the dean, whose office door faces mine across the hall, only to be assured that I was hardly *in loco parentis*, so should assume no responsibility for the apparel of those who came for scholastic help. Nevertheless, I was somewhat relieved when cooler weather seemed to take care of the matter.

About the second week, she complained of headaches that recurred a couple or three times each day for no explainable reason.

"Everything's OK till I take the boys to school. It seems that by the time I leave them off I begin to get sharp throbbing pains in my head, and by the time I get to my own classes, I feel like screaming."

About the third or fourth week I asked her whether she had had any hang-ups about leaving the boys before. Negative, except when she had driven the boys to see their father, as she was obligated to do each month.

"That produces a real king-sized headache, but I understand why—Ichabod thinks visiting privileges extend to the boys *and* their mother, and I can get pretty up-tight about that. In fact, my head nearly killed me when I left them there on Friday, and again on the way back on Sunday. But my frustrations with that clown can easily explain those headaches. *He* always was a headache!"

At my suggestion, she saw a doctor, who tried various medications, to no avail. The pain hit her every time she left her boys off or took them home—even sometimes when she came to school without them.

I was reminded of a sheriff I knew who was

troubled by stomach cramps, and ultimately bleeding ulcers. His doctor tried to relate the condition to stress on the job—dealing with bank robbers, fugitives, emergencies of all kinds—but somehow the correlation was poor. One day the lawman said, "Doc, it's crazy, but every time I turn into my driveway, I get a sharp cramp in my belly. How come?"

Whereupon the good physician asked a few questions about the home.

"Well, my wife's got to be the sloppiest woman on earth. I have to kick a path through the trash just to cross the room. And at 6:00 P.M. she's still in her housecoat, her hair looking like the unmade beds upstairs. Believe me, I come home as late as possible."

Eventually the man got a divorce, and the ulcers became merely a part of the bad memory. The name of the game is psychosomatic illness, and I draped the term neatly over the divorcee and her headaches. But what did they all have to do with taking the kids to and from school, and going to classes at the college? Not being a physician, I concluded that some hidden chemical or organic deficiency was being triggered in some esoteric way, and tried to encourage her to think positively and place the trials of the day in the hands of the Lord.

Soon after Thanksgiving she dropped in for her usual visit, and as usual I asked her how everything was doing.

"Just great. Did well in all the midterms. Oh, by the way—no more headaches! How about that?"

"Hey, that's wonderful. The doctor finally figured them out, huh? Or did you?"

"Actually, neither. I was taking the boys to their father's for Thanksgiving when the younger one suddenly said, 'Mom, this car stinks!' And then it hit me—the muffler was a bit noisy, so maybe exhaust gas was getting into the car. My head was splitting as usual, and I was more than eager for relief. So I stopped at the first service station and asked the man to check it. One look under the car, and he said, 'Lady, you and them kids is lucky to be alive!' I let him know it wasn't luck; the good Lord had protected me and the boys from my own stupidity. Now, with a new muffler on the car, I have no more headaches when I haul the boys to school, or even when I go to Ichabod's place."

So much for my diagnostic skill . . .

CHAPTER 10

I *LIKE* TO BE SHOCKED

Pondering the humbling experience of failing to detect the obvious cause of the divorcee's headaches, I tend to become progressively more nondirective in my contacts with young people.

For instance, there was June. Upper-division student. Good character, immaculate in personal grooming. Lots of friends, but few dates—and that was the rub. Our discussions revealed that she was quite attracted to John, a fellow student who walked her home from the observatory once a week after astronomy class and liked to talk with her at other times.

I asked her to tell me about John, and she seemed to be less than specific about his character. In fact, in the first few conversations she didn't mention his name. When it was convenient, I asked what they found to talk about during those protracted visits. Seeing that she avoided that question, I asked who seemed to choose the topics. Well, he seemed to guide things, but he was so well informed (and she was really only a small-town girl) that she just thought it was great to listen and get her eyes opened about so many things.

"You sort of feel that he's been around a lot, and

he's filling you in on some things you've missed."

"Yes. And he has read everything. He gets almost straight A's, too. I have always admired a keen mind, and he certainly has one."

"Do you agree with his ideas on most things?"

"Well, no. But that's what makes him interesting. Actually, he's got some real way-out ideas about religion, and I'm pretty conservative, but he says we don't mature by shutting ourselves off from other viewpoints."

"Would you say he's a Christian?"

"No. He's very honest. Makes no claims. He calls himself a seeker. As I said, some things he comes up with really shock me."

"Do you like to be shocked?"

"Well, yes, and I'm sure he thinks it's great to shock little innocent me. But don't get the wrong idea. He knows better than to try any funny stuff, 'cause I've told him where I stand. We just talk."

At another visit she admitted that he "kinda scares me sometimes."

"Would you say that when you're with John you get the feeling you're playing with fire?"

"Yes, but let's face it—I *like* to play with fire. And besides, I always keep control of the situation. He knows what I stand for. I'd never marry someone like John, if that's what you're worried about. He's too coarse and unrefined. I just admire his sharp mind, I guess. That's the only reason I can think of for spending so much time talking to him. I really don't even consider him a social equal."

At another session: "You know, June, psychologists suggest that girls tend to choose partners with the traits of their fathers. What is your dad like?"

I could see I had touched a tender nerve.

"John and my dad are complete opposites. John

admits he doesn't have conventional moral standards, and Daddy is as faithful a husband as there is. I *know* he's true to Mother. But I don't want to marry a carbon copy of my dad, much as I love him."

Here it looked like impending tears, so I pushed the box of Kleenex across the desk and waited for her to gain composure. It wasn't easy. Finally she began talking again, looking off into space.

"The trouble with Dad is he has no refinement, and Mother is so cultured. He has no consideration for her feelings, no sensitivity. I love him, but he has dragged her down to his own crude level, or tried to."

More tears. Because it was time for her next class, that ended the conversation, but in a few days she was back, having done some reflective thinking. She picked up where we had left off.

"There is some truth about your hint that I like John because he has some of Dad's traits. But really they're actually so different. Daddy is very careful of what he talks about in front of my sister and me; but John blurts out anything without blushing, and when I scold him he just laughs at me. And don't worry about his leading me astray—he's never even suggested a date."

"But suppose he were to turn romantic some moonlit evening—how susceptible would you be?"

"John is incapable of being romantic. That's why I'm safe with him. He has said many times that he doesn't believe in love. He thinks love and sex have no relation to each other. And I'm pretty old-fashioned on that score. So there's nothing to worry about. You think he might change my thinking, I know, but it would be impossible for me to get involved in a crude liaison such as he would offer. So quit worrying."

It was some weeks later, in the spring of the year, when a very disturbed June sat across the desk.

"Get out the Kleenex, please."

I complied, and awaited the outburst. It came. "You know something? I was face to face with death this afternoon. Not just a crude proposition. Not just rape, but murder!" And the sobs shook her like a mouse in the teeth of a cat.

"John suggested a walk, and it was a beautiful day, so I went. When we were well back along the trail, he said he thought it was time we quit acting like Sunday school kids and satisfied our basic needs, since we knew each other well, et cetera. I was shocked and told him so. He couldn't see why I was so stunned, and said I should have expected it. Then he tried to put his ideas into action, but I was pretty wild myself by then, and he got some nasty scratches.

"When he calmed down and gave up the battle, we started walking back, saying nothing. But when we came along a ledge with a ten- or fifteen-foot drop to the rocks, he stopped and looked down. His face turned red, and he growled, 'June, no girl has ever refused me and gotten away with it. I feel like killing you, and here's a good place to do it.' Mr. Aaen, I never prayed so hard in my life."

Those prayers must have been effective, for here she sat, weeping tears of panic, terror, shame, and gratitude that she was alive. There wasn't much to say, so I waited till she had subsided, and together we thanked God for her deliverance. Nor did I ever attempt to point up the moral of the story. Ultimately she herself summarized the whole episode and drew the obvious conclusions. Perhaps I should have foreseen the real dangers and warned her more explicitly. But would she have accepted the warning?

CHAPTER 11

ENVIRONMENT IS NO EXCUSE

Why do some young people from a sheltered Christian home, like June, seem so attracted by friends who are obviously worldly and cynical? Sometimes just the opposite holds true.

Trisha first came to my office to explain why a freshman theme was late. She had had a chance for some extra work, and just could not pass it up. Having but limited financial resources, she had to earn every cent possible to avoid overstepping her no-extras budget. In response to my question about her parents, she assured me there was no chance for help from her mother or stepfather.

"You see, Daddy hasn't really worked steady since he married Mother, when I was about 6 years old. He has always complained of poor health, but he just drinks too much. He's really not a good man, either, so of course I get no help from home."

From time to time she would drop in for help on a theme, and I began to admire her serious but cheerful approach to life. Gradually she began to talk about herself, and I learned that some years previously her mother had taken the children to church, but eventually she herself quit attending. Kind friends paid to keep the children in church school—as long as they wanted to go. One by one the others dropped out and went to the nearby public school, but not Trisha. Her home was in the San Francisco slums, and the local elementary school was in every sense a ghetto school, so Trisha preferred a Christian education, in spite of the long trip each day.

One day while visiting in my office, she mentioned having left home at the age of 12, and I asked her why.

"Frankly, I couldn't stand my stepdad. He wouldn't keep his hands off me."

"Why didn't you tell your mother?"

"You won't believe this, but Mother never sympathized with me. She said he didn't mean any harm, and I should think nothing of it. So one day I just went to the home of one of the church members and phoned Mother that I would be staying there. She didn't seem to mind, and though I went home for frequent visits, she never urged me to move back. I just somehow didn't fit into that life style."

She surely didn't. Sweet Christian purity shone about her like a halo, even though she must hardly have been naive, having worked for room and board in several homes, and attended an inner-city high school for two years. Subsequent to high school graduation she worked as a secretary for a San Francisco business firm before coming to Pacific Union College.

Once, when submitting a paper, she said, rather apologetically, "This isn't a very good theme, and I know it. I'm just not all that smart. My grades have always been C's, with an occasional B; never an A. But I study hard, and get all my assignments in. I do wish, though, that I had the brains of some of these other kids."

If smartness is farsightedness, if intelligence is

the ability to make the right decision, if wisdom is the knack of putting first things first, I would rate this girl one of the wisest I have met. I submit that hell will be awash with brilliant fools. Further, when by the grace of God I enter that eternal realm, I expect to see Trisha's quiet smile.

Predictably, Trisha's brother was frequently afoul of the law. He wrote her once, while awaiting trial on a car-theft charge, so she wrote a long letter, pleading with him to accept Christ's forgiveness, and change his friends and his way of life. That letter was intercepted by the district attorney and read in court, with the admonition that if his sister could rise above her environment, he could too.

She agonized over the slovenly conduct of her two young sisters, and from her meager earnings sent them gifts of clothing and Bibles and other good reading matter. Their usual response was to tell her how stuffy her way of life was, and how much fun they were having.

Trisha's wholesome charm did not go unnoticed on the campus, and eventually she found herself more than casually responsive to one of her fellow upperclassmen. Although her early home experiences had left a residue of what to her were quite puzzling reactions (to the extent that she really had to force herself to take her escort's arm when walking into a concert), prayer and counsel helped her to see that she must not react to a serious suitor as she had to a repulsive and morally sick stepfather.

Trisha was a beautiful bride, and her wedding was simple, but lovely. As she and her husband came to tell me of their call to the mission field, and as I observed their obvious love for each other and their Lord, I could only praise God for this continuing miracle.

In this context, the story of Josiah comes to mind. He was the son of Amon, grandson of Manasseh, two of Judah's wickedest kings. Their court was hardly an ideal place for the infancy of a great godly reformer. The blood bath that wiped out his father and set the boy on the throne at a tender age testified to the extent of the corruption of that court. But 2 Kings 22:2 says that Josiah did that which was right in the eyes of the Lord, and that he did not turn aside to the right or the left.

Daniel, Joseph, Josiah, and others proved long ago that corrupt surroundings provide no excuse for indulging in immorality. Jesus ("Can there any good thing come out of Nazareth?") reinforced the principle, and Trisha underlined it for our generation.

CHAPTER 12

THE COUNSELOR AS CUPID

There *are* delightful episodes in the memory of any counselor, whether he counsels full time or part time. There are always a few Trishas—and a few Margarets.

Margaret had never sat in one of my classes, but I knew her casually and had met her parents. At the beginning of her senior year she and a friend, whom I knew much better, stopped by my office. After an exchange of pleasantries that were obviously designed to lead into something more important, Margaret's friend got to the point: she had brought Margaret in because she needed to discuss a matter, and was hesitant to come alone.

"Really, Mr. Aaen, I'm here only because Helen insisted. I said I'd like to get some advice on sort of a silly matter that a college senior should know how to handle."

"No problem is silly or little if it upsets you. So I'll not laugh. And let's not say you're here to get advice; let's just say you need help in seeing the problem—and its possible solutions—clearly. Then, of course, *you* must choose from among the alternatives. OK?"

"OK. But I still don't know how to say what's bugging me."

"Well, Margaret, I'm sure I can't guess. Since you have lovely parents, it's not likely to be a family problem."

"Oh, no. My folks are the greatest."

"And how are things going spiritually?"

"Fine; I've never felt closer to the Lord."

"Grades OK?"

"So-so. Mostly B's."

"I thought so. And socially you seem to be in an enviable position—constantly escorted by an up-and-coming theology major of good character and good family, who just happens to drive a flashy car."

"That's just where the problem lies—I mean, sure he's nice to have around, and lots of girls envy me, but——"

"But what?"

"But he keeps wanting to get serious."

"That's bad?"

"Well, no. But frankly, I'm not all that interested."

"And you'd like out of the arrangement."

"Yes, I guess that's it. He bugs me lately."

"What bugs you? Anything specific?"

"Just little things. Like he doesn't open the car door for me, and he doesn't stand when a lady comes to the table, and sometimes he comes to the cafeteria with dirty fingernails."

"A fellow could have worse faults, you know. What if he'd correct these irritating traits? Then how would you feel?"

"I'd still want to quit. What I really want to know is how to drop him painlessly. That's my whole problem. Got any suggestions?"

"Has someone else got your eye?"

"No one in particular, but after all, George is the only fellow I've dated in college. Maybe there *could* be someone else. How do I know?"

We then listed George's good points—and they were considerable—versus his drawbacks, none of which was really serious. She agreed that most girls would consider her lucky, but insisted she still wanted to break up with him. The question was how to do it. I assured her that a "Dear John" letter would be cowardly, since she was on the same campus with him, so a face-to-face confrontation was better. I also explained that his first response would be "Why? What have I done?" The only honest, and decisive, answer would be to state emphatically, "I've just lost interest." This is completely frustrating and exasperating to the fellow, but it also has one virtue—it's unanswerable, unassailable, and therefore effective. And that was her objective—a clean break.

"As sure as you give him one reason—his manners, for instance—you place yourself in an untenable position. He'll take a cram course in the social graces, then say, 'OK, now I've corrected the problem, so you must take me back,' and then you're stuck. You probably still won't want him. So remember, if you mean business, give him no reasons; just say you want out of the deal. Period."

"But that sounds so cruel. I don't want to hurt him. He's really been great to me."

"This is a situation in which an honest statement is the kindest one. Would you want a boyfriend who kept on with you only because he didn't want to hurt your feelings by telling you he was tired of you?"

We had a word of prayer, and Margaret left my office. I wondered whether I had said the right thing.

Two or three days later George stopped in. His visible distress indicated that Margaret had spoken her piece. Somehow I had not expected *him* to come, so I braced myself for what I feared would be an accusation of betrayal. To my great relief, he seemed not to know Margaret had been in to see me.

Without much overture, he got to the core of his problem.

"What do you do when a girl drops you just like that—and won't even give you a reason?"

Feeling just a slight bit sneaky, I said, "Sounds as though something happened between you and Margaret."

"You know it. She's been acting funny for the past couple weeks, and then yesterday she said she just wanted to break up—just like that. And she won't give me a *reason*. Is that fair?"

"Well, George, she may not *have* a reason, or at least one that would seem logical to a male mind. Women don't always think logically—they are more likely to come to intuitive conclusions. Which, of course, is of little comfort to your bruised ego."

"My ego isn't the problem. I just can't see why she should all of a sudden dump me, without giving me a chance to correct whatever it is that she thinks is wrong. A guy ought to have a chance to fight back, to defend himself, or something. Is there something wrong with me? If so, I have a right to know. Actually, I think her friend Helen is at the bottom of this, though I never did *her* any harm."

When he had subsided a bit, I asked him whether he really wanted Margaret back or if he just wanted vengeance. He assured me he had no wish but to win her love. Since one scarcely knows his own heart, to say nothing of another's, I assured him it was useless to try to account for why girls did this or that. However, he might, by careful planning, assist her in gaining some insights that would be helpful to her and to his own cause.

Margaret had learned to depend on his concern

for her, and had doubtless found his devotion a real support to her ego, to the point that she perhaps took it for granted. He might help her to realize that his love for her was valuable by denying it to her.

"But Mr. Aaen, she doesn't care about my love, or she would not have given me the boot."

"Listen, George, she doesn't really think you'll withdraw your love. She thinks it will always be available. Not that she's cynical—she probably never reasoned it that way at all. But the fact remains that unless some knight on a white steed charges in to fill the vacancy, she's going to need to know you're available. If you hang around like a faithful sheep dog, she has her reassurance, and you have nothing. She has no real incentive to examine her attachment to you."

"So what do you suggest? I can't just forget her, like that. Habit, if nothing else, is hard to change."

"You can do what you wish, but I should point out one advantage that fellows have. You can date at will, whereas girls have to wait till someone asks them. Since she has said that she wants to be free, take her at her word. Treat her as you would any other girl—casually. Don't stop to talk. Don't stare at her. Be friendly with other girls, and don't give her the impression you're waiting for her to change her mind."

"Do you mean I should date somebody else? I don't *want* to date anyone else. *She's* the one I love. None of these other girls look good to me."

"OK, OK, I know that, but if anything will make you look valuable to Margaret, it will be the realization that you can get along without her. Plus, it will be good for your own soul not to mope around. So sharpen up the old etiquette and social skills, like opening doors for the ladies and being especially careful about your personal appearance. Then either Margaret will reconsider or you'll find you're having so much fun you won't care."

He left my office with a plan of action, if not a lot of optimism. Admittedly, I felt uncomfortable—a bit deceitful, in fact—about holding the confidence of both sides in this little drama (not little to them, but actually only a tiny subplot in the drama that seethes and permeates any college campus), but since I had been honest with both parties, I decided to forget it, after placing the whole matter in the Lord's hands. Neither George nor Margaret ever returned for counsel.

In the spring quarter I saw George drive by, with Margaret sitting beside him as though there were two or three invisible passengers crowding her against him. Later, as I met them arm in arm at a concert, each flashed me a mysterious, conspiratorial smile. The following autumn my wife and I received an invitation to their wedding, which, alas, we were unable to attend.

Though our paths have never crossed, they have kept us posted on their call to the mission field, and arrival of children. Sometimes I have wondered, Did they have a big laugh as they compared notes about those two visits in my office in Irwin Hall? Did George actually date other girls? Did Margaret make the first overture toward reconciliation? Do they recall these events as I do? All these questions are really quite irrelevant, since to all appearances the outcome has been a happy Christian family, busy in the service of the Lord.

CHAPTER 13

THE EMPTY MAILBOX

One aspect of boarding-school life that gets, alas, all too little attention from parents is the letter from home. Everyone has heard of the student who seldom writes home, unless perhaps to ask for money, and doubtless there are too many children who neglect their long-suffering parents in this way.

On the other hand, serious inroads have been made on my Kleenex supply by girls whose parents leave them with empty mailboxes day after day. Boys have other ways of working off their frustrations at uncommunicative parents, but the sense of alienation is nonetheless real.

From the stories I've listened to, I think I could fashion a fairly accurate profile of the nonwriting mother. First, she is almost without fail a career woman, very much involved with her profession. Second, she is proud of her son or daughter. At least to hear her talk about the child and how much she and her spouse are spending to keep the offspring in school, you feel there's just nothing they wouldn't do for their little Iodine or Egbert. And verily, they *do* usually provide well—perhaps Iodine wears the best clothes in school. But there is something about that motherly career that saps all the strength of this visibly fond parent, so little or no energy is left for writing encouraging notes. Many in this category occasionally pick up the phone and call, but more often it is little lonesome Iodine who phones collect. The calls are likely to go something like this:

"Hello, Mother, is everything all right at home?"

"Of course, darling. Why do you ask?"

"Well, you haven't written, and I was worried."

"Why, child, I just wrote you."

"But, Mom, that was three weeks ago. And that means I've been to the empty mailbox eighteen times now."

"You *know* I'd write if anything went wrong. Daddy and I are so busy. Just don't worry; I'll write if there is any problem. You're a big girl now, and it's just a little while till Thanksgiving vacation."

"But, Mother, that's nearly three weeks yet. How is my dog? And did you get the kitchen painted? You know, I get to wondering how things are at home sometimes. Are my goldfish OK?"

"Silly girl, everything is OK. The kitchen is just the same as when you left. We feed the dog and the goldfish faithfully. Just don't worry about things. When you feel homesick, call us, dear. Now I have to go, honey. I'll write when I get time."

"'Bye, Mother. Tell Dad hello."

Maria had come 400 miles to college, with her parents' consent if not their support. Since her folks were not church members, the local Adventist church was paying her expenses. When she came in, at my invitation, to discuss some overdue essays, I learned that she was having difficulty adjusting to dormitory life and the college regime—hardly a unique problem. Suspecting an unstated cause, I asked a few questions, and soon had an all-too-familiar, tearful story.

In nearly three months she had received not one letter from her family. Desperately she had called home and even the shop where her father worked, where she received matter-of-fact answers to her questions, and finally a cutoff, because of a caller on the other line. At Thanksgiving time she had phoned for permission to fly home, and her Dad said, "Sure, just call when you get to the airport." Didn't even ask what flight. She tried to bolster her sorely strained sense of filial respect by telling herself how generous her family was to fly her home, when most of her friends had to ride eight hours in cars. Excitedly she phoned as soon as she landed, and was told that someone would be out to the airport "in a little while." Two snail-paced hours later she phoned again, only to be told that Mother and Dad and sister and brother-in-law were all pretty busy; she perhaps had better take a cab, and they'd pay for it when she got there. Once home, she dropped easily into the family routine, but no one seemed interested in her life at the college. Daddy did take her to the airport, but couldn't stay to see her off. Now it was approaching Christmas, and Maria was still hurrying to the dorm from classes at midday to see if there might *just once* be a letter.

"If just once *they'd* call *me* or even send a silly card. Why do I always have to call *them?* I've quit writing them, but there's no evidence it makes any difference to them. I even hate myself for going to my mailbox every day, when I know there won't be anything in it."

What can a counselor say to a situation like that? All my excuses and rationalizations still added up to just one stark fact to Maria—her family just didn't care much. No wonder she had difficulty keeping her attention on her studies. Three years later Maria, a much more poised young lady, planned and directed a mother-daughter banquet at the college. It was beautiful. The only criticism I heard was that the mother-daughter relationship was oversentimentalized. As she introduced her very proud mother to me the next day, I just wondered if her message had gotten across.

Linda had the same problem, but tended to rationalize by saying her mother was a stepmother, and both parents were busy physicians. Nevertheless, she was hypnotized by the mailbox—just couldn't pass it up, though she knew it would be empty. I kept telling her that at 19 years of age she should be mature enough to find other resources to keep up her spirits. Although really an attractive young woman, she couldn't keep a steady boyfriend. Ironically, she knew what the problem was—she was too possessive, too eager, and the fellows felt threatened by her. Her rather candid self-appraisal was "I'm a warm, affectionate person. Emotionally I'm power-packed, and the man I marry better be ready for lots of loving."

"How do you know, Linda? What makes you think you are any more affectionate than the next person, other than the fact that you have never had opportunity to express your emotions?" She was reluctant to concede that the only difference between her and the next girl was a certain emotional deprivation, but at least I tried to make that point.

Spring vacation found the campus almost devoid of dorm students, but to my surprise I saw Linda at church, alone and red-eyed. In response to my question she said, with all the sincerity she could muster, "No, I couldn't go home this vacation. The folks phoned early in the week to say they were awfully sorry but they had had unexpected expenses and just couldn't afford the plane fare. You know, Dad is working on a specialty, and women doctors never make as much as the men do."

I wanted to shed a few tears right there in front of the church myself. She was trying so heroically to believe their excuse, when she and I both knew the truth all too well—her presence at home just simply wouldn't be convenient.

When Linda did get a steady boyfriend, she predictably and literally clung to him morning, noon, and night. Because both students and teachers were joking about her PDA (public display of affection) and because I felt a real concern, I spoke to her as tactfully as I could. Someway I got the impression I would have been more successful if I had snatched a cub from its mother. To put it mildly, my well-intended intervention was not appreciated. Fortunately for Linda, the lad could absorb a lot of smothering, and in due time they were married, albeit not at her home church. I had the suspicion that the marriage at the college was less disturbing to the family.

Linda could easily have fallen prey to some of the snares that await girls whose emotional needs are not met by loving parents and who substitute unscrupulous, promise-them-anything fellows for the empty mailbox, which dramatizes in "technicolor, wide screen" the tragic fact that to their own parents they just aren't very important.

It was David who said, "No man cared for my soul."

CHAPTER 14

BRIDE FOR SALE

A school administrator in an alien culture faces all the problems he would at home, plus others exotic enough to satisfy his yen for the new and different for a lifetime. Especially is this true when he becomes involved in marriage matters.

School was nearly out at our junior college in Java. One afternoon I walked into the back of the typing room, my footsteps muffled by the rattle of the typewriters of two or three students practicing for tomorrow's speed tests. Stepping up behind Sorva, I noticed that she was not copying what was on her book, but was composing as she typed. Fascinated, I read enough to learn that she was to return home to an arranged marriage with a man she hardly knew. Not wishing to intrude, I tiptoed out, unnoticed.

A few days later I watched Sorva, with the help of a friend, carry her suitcase and trunk out to the bus, tears staining her cheeks. Impulse said that I should rush out and tell her not to go, that she would never be happy married to someone she didn't love. But better judgment said that arranged marriages have been the custom for ages in the East, and who was I to flaunt local tradition? In discussions with our local pastors I had been reminded that Western romantic courtship had not produced a great deal of marriage stability either.

Later during the vacation period I learned that Sorva had flatly refused to go through with the marriage, on the grounds that she was too young. I suppose she was 16 or 17 at the time. Actually, her handicap was that she was much prettier than the average of her people, so she was much sought after. In a culture where the bride's father collects a gift from the groom's family, there is a strong tendency to favor the man who offers the highest bid rather than the one who will make the most considerate husband.

Acting as though I had heard nothing about the planned marriage or the change of plans, I wrote Sorva an encouraging letter, telling her the school looked forward to seeing her when we opened again in September.

To our great joy she did return in the fall, to finish her prenursing course. Although never a brilliant student, she was accepted for nurse's training for the following year.

During that school year, Wilson, one of our senior ministerial students, dropped into my office. After introducing several topics that he and I both understood were merely polite but meaningless preliminaries, he got down to business.

"Elder Aaen, you know I am graduating and looking for a call to the ministry. I know that any mission that calls me will expect me either to be married or to have definite marriage plans. Right?"

"Yes, Wilson, that is true. I guess they consider a single pastor incompetent to counsel married people; perhaps they think he's too vulnerable, as well."

I could have added also that local custom denied

respect to an unmarried man. The idea seemed to be that maturity was somehow bestowed when in the marriage ceremony the pastor pronounced those special words.

I continued, "What do you have in mind as a remedy for this important deficiency? I don't recall seeing you very friendly with any of our girls here on the campus. Is there someone at home that you are negotiating with?"

"Well, no, no one at home. But perhaps you could help me arrange things here at the school. I have Sorva in mind."

I nearly blurted out, "So do half the other fellows on campus," but instead I managed, "But, Wilson, I've never even seen you talking to her. Is she aware of your interest?"

The truth was that Sorva had so many admirers that she might be excused for not noticing one or two. The fellows swarmed around her like bees around the honeysuckle. Wilson was a good boy, but hardly the kind to set an extremely popular girl's heart thumping.

"It's true we are never together, because all those other guys get in the way, but our villages are near each other in Sumatra, and I have asked my father to arrange it all with her father. So really, Sorva will have little to say in the matter. And once we are married, those guys won't dare come near her; I'll see to that. And I think she knows what her future is, although she doesn't let on to me that her parents have said anything." Wilson spoke confidently.

"Yes, but she is just finishing lower middle school, and you are graduating as a minister. Do you want a half-educated wife? She's planning to go into nursing in August. I doubt that she'll give up her education and career now. That doesn't make sense."

"That's where you come in, Elder Aaen. I want you to talk to her on my behalf. I need her, and I love her, and in time I'm sure she will love me too. All I need is your help in convincing her."

"But you must understand, Wilson, that I have no idea whether you and Sorva are suited to each other or not. Even if I were certain, what makes you think she would listen to me any more than to you? Furthermore, *you* are the one she will be living with for the rest of her life, not me. In the first place, I don't think she's mature enough for marriage, and in the second place, I see no evidence that she loves you. You are just going to have to approach her yourself. I suggest that you make this a matter of prayer, being certain that you can accept the Lord's answer, no matter what that may be."

We had prayer, and he left, more than slightly disappointed at my lack of enthusiasm for his cause. And I was convinced he would be sending me no valentine next February.

Two or three days later, Sorva sat across the desk from me, very serious and thoughtful. It just did not seem right to see her without that radiant smile.

"And what can your problem be, Sorva? Is someone in your family sick?" (I had a fair idea, but preferred to let her introduce the subject.)

"Elder Aaen, you know I want to do the Lord's will, and that I have always wanted to be a nurse. Is it selfish for me to go ahead with nursing now, when duty calls me to do something else? I don't want to be selfish."

I may not be the smartest of God's creatures, but from somewhere in the foggy recesses of my mind lurked the shadow of Wilson.

"What is selfish about taking the nurse's course? And what duty could be more important than caring

76

for the sick and suffering?"

"Well, Wilson can't go into the ministry unless I marry him. I've had letters from his family and from mine. My father has already agreed with his father on the bridal gift, and Wilson is really pressuring me. I don't want to hinder the Lord's work, but I really do want to be a nurse. Wilson reminds me that I should honor what my parents say, according to the fifth commandment." Her eyes filled, and frustration and disappointment marked her every look and gesture.

"Wait a minute, Sorva. Who says Wilson has to have *you* in order to get a call to the ministry? There are other girls, you know. He may prefer you, but that's his problem, not yours. Also, the Lord's work needs good nurses as well as good preachers' wives."

Somehow I bristled inwardly at Wilson's tactics, which I considered unfair, and at the haste of Sorva's father to collect a fat marriage price for his unusually attractive daughter, which I interpreted as greed.

"But Elder Aaen, how about my parents? I really upset them last summer by refusing to marry that other man. Now they point out that Wilson is young, well educated, and will be a respected professional. Also, they keep reminding me of the fifth commandment."

"Sorva, I want to ask you one question. Would your parents urge you to marry Wilson if his father were not promising several water buffalos and a lot of cash?"

"Of course not. My father has debts that he expects to pay off when I marry. He needs the money."

"So then your father is not thinking of what is good for you, but is mostly concerned about his own finances and needs."

"Yes, I guess you're right."

"Do you think Wilson is primarily concerned about the Lord's work, or about his own personal preference?"

"Oh, I've known for years that Wilson likes me. It's just that I always thought he was blah, and I still do."

"And don't you think parents should respect their children in order to be worthy of their children's respect?"

"To tell the truth, it has always bothered me to hear that so-and-so got so many buffalos for his daughter; but that's our custom, and we just submit to it without question. Deep within me I know my folks are happy that I'm pretty, because I'll bring a big marriage price. I really don't think they are very concerned whether I'm happy or not."

Then came the shocker. "Elder Aaen, I don't know what to do. Will you decide for me? If you say No, I'll say No; and if you tell me to go ahead, I'll do it. This decision is too much for me."

"Wait a minute! Who is going to have to live with this man 365 days a year—you or me? If he leads you astray, who faces the judgment? I have advised a number of young folks *not* to marry this person or that person, but I refuse to say they *should* marry anyone. As far as Wilson is concerned, I think he's a fine young Christian, but I have no way of knowing what kind of husband he will be. If you want to marry him, I will not discourage you. But I will not make the decision for you. There is a source of help in this situation, and that is prayer. The Lord will impress you if you ask Him to. He is concerned about your happiness. His judgment is not influenced by buffalos and cash. Ask Him, and be willing to accept His promptings."

We had prayer, and she left, still with the burden

of decision. I would like to have said what I felt she should do and relieve her of having to choose, but it is never the counselor's prerogative to decide. Ultimately the counselee must learn to accept responsibility for his actions so he cannot say, "This was really my pastor's [or teacher's or parent's] decision, not mine; so I can't be blamed for the results."

What went through Sorva's mind after that, I don't know, but I'm sure she prayed. I never saw her with Wilson, but one way or another she got the message to him—she would *not* marry him.

However, if I thought the Sorva story was closed, I was wrong. At the end of the school term, most of the students accepted for nurse's training hurried home for a visit during the four-week interval before classes began at the hospital. Sorva and two friends lived so far away that it was impractical for them to go home. Boats were too slow and air fare too expensive. So we notified their parents that arrangements had been made for them to stay at the home of Dr. and Mrs. Jess Holm, near the hospital, until they could enter the nurses' dormitory. In each case, the parents agreed.

During examination week Sorva came to my office, red-eyed and distraught, and showed me a telegram from her father, saying simply that she was to return home as soon as school was out.

"Yes, Sorva, I know. I have a telegram from your father also, saying you are to come home. What do you think is behind this? Is he still trying to marry you to Wilson?"

"Oh, no. That was all settled months ago. Wilson has someone else in mind. A girlfriend with whom I worked last vacation keeps me posted on things at home. This time my dad really revealed his motives about me. A rich Moslem about 40 years old, who already has a wife and kids, has offered a huge sum for me, and I guess Dad couldn't resist. What can I do? You've got to help me. Compared to the two other guys, this one is awful. At least the others were single and Christians. This fellow is a married Moslem. What do I do?"

"OK, Sorva, since your dad does not explain why he wants you home, let's assume he just wants to see you before you begin studying at the hospital. Wait two or three days, and write him that you appreciate his wanting you to come home before starting the nurse's course, but that you've talked it over with the president of the school, and that I've checked the boat schedules and there's just no way for you to make it to your village and back in four weeks. Thank him profusely, and tell him how much you would like to see him and your mother, and how grateful you are for their helping you get your education. I will wait a few days and write your parents, explaining that there are no boat schedules that would get you there and back in the time you are free. By the time he receives our letters and responds, you will already be studying at the hospital."

And that's what we did. Her father knew she would never come if he told her his plans for her, so he had to accept the explanation we wrote him. On the other hand, I could imagine his frustration at seeing a fortune slip away, while he was powerless to do anything about it.

Sorva had to struggle with her studies, but caring for the sick was a gift she had in abundance. The patients loved her, and she loved them. After finishing the three years of training she stayed on to work at the hospital, and proved so efficient that she was given administrative responsibility. On one occasion when one doctor was on furlough and the other one was called away for two days, it was Sorva who was placed in charge of the entire hospital—inpatient, outpatient, and business functions. She had poise and charm that seemed to melt difficulty.

Later on when Dr. Holm was invited to conduct a series of clinics in the villages of North Sumatra, the logical choice for nurse-translator was, of course, Sorva. One unsolicited volunteer handyman, who accompanied the team from village to village (including Sorva's own), was her very proud father, who never missed an opportunity to announce that the beautiful nurse in the starched uniform was his daughter.

She had come a long way from the frightened little girl whose tears fell on her typewriter six or seven years earlier. She had made her own decisions, with the help of the Lord.

CHAPTER 15

IS IT FAIR TO LET HIM FALL FOR ME?

On the other side of the Pacific, a few years later, another charming young woman faced the problem of choosing a life partner, though her situation—along with her cultural background—was different from that of Sorva.

"Well, Judy, you look happy today. Is it the spring flowers and the beauty of nature, or has some young Galahad smiled?"

"Some of both, I suppose. But I don't exactly know what to do about him."

"Fortunately, or unfortunately, society has decreed that there isn't much for a young lady to do. Just be friendly, keep that charming smile, and nature will take care of the rest."

"But, no kidding, this guy is neat. He's a good Christian, a senior, and he wants to be a missionary. Why should he look at me? I mean, is it fair to let him flip like this?"

"And why not? You're more attractive than the average. You're only a sophomore, but you're 21. You're a prayer-band leader. I see no reason for you to feel inferior. Let him fall!"

I knew Judy through my family. About a year previous, my wife had gone to San Francisco on a shopping trip. Feeling hungry, she decided to look for a restaurant. Market Street, where she was walking, has many eating places, so she uttered a simple, rather perfunctory prayer, asking the Lord to help her find a good place to eat. She found herself in a Chinese-American restaurant, and frankly, the food was disappointing. Not far away sat a pretty girl, obviously studying while she ate. When the girl had paid and was walking out, my wife, with no particular motive, asked her, "What language were the folks using at the next table? Did you understand it?"

"No. It intrigued me, but it didn't sound like anything I'd ever heard. May I ask you a question? Do you have a daughter named Peggy?"

"Why, yes. Do you know her?"

"Of course; I'm Judy ———. We went to the academy together a few years ago."

"Peggy regretted many times that she lost track of you, Judy. She'd love to see you."

Judy said that she was attending San Francisco State University, living with friends in the city. My wife took her address, and when Peggy came home from Loma Linda a couple weeks later, she wrote Judy a letter, inviting her to come and visit for a few days. Judy didn't write her answer; she phoned, saying she'd come on Friday. Though she planned a weekend, her stay extended to a week, during which time we did our best to sell her on PUC for the fall.

Aside from a clever bread-and-butter letter, we heard nothing from Judy during the summer; but when registration came around in September, there she was, standing in line. Since she was an English major, I helped her line up her schedule, and from time to time she would drop by the office and say Hello.

One sunny day she seemed radiant, and I asked why all the smiles. Her explanation went this way:

"Friday night my roommate was away, and I was lonesome. I wondered what I was doing at this place anyway. I'd been here a month and, really, the only friend I had was my roommate. At San Francisco State I had plenty of friends, and plenty of dates. Rather mechanically I got ready and walked down to vespers, pitying myself because no one was friendly. S.F. State was going to get a student second quarter, for sure. With the other kids, I filed into the church and sank down in a back seat. Could anyone else possibly feel as lonesome and blue as I did?

"Just then I looked up, and there stood a girl, all by herself, looking for a place to sit—really for someone to sit with. Suddenly I thought, Here's someone who needs a friend as much as I do, and I motioned her to sit beside me. Her response was a big smile and a sigh of relief as she joined me.

"After the service, as we walked back to the dorm, she told me I'd never know how much my little gesture meant, for she was lonesome and loaded with self-pity. Taking my cue from something the speaker had said, I invited her to my room for a word of prayer before she went to bed.

"Would you believe that that was my first prayer since I quit the academy five years before? But it was wonderful to feel I was of help to someone. All week now I've been going out of my way to smile and to cheer up girls who look discouraged. And I feel great. Prayer is a new and exhilarating experience. You'll never know how glad I am that your wife spoke to me in that restaurant, and that I accepted the invitation to come to college here."

When the Week of Prayer came, Judy was ready. She was an active participant in a very profound religious revival on the campus, a dynamic influence for good.

And now it was spring, and the love bug had bitten her. I could see no reason for her to be worried, but she was. Finally she said, "Is it fair to let a nice guy like Joe fall for me when I've made such a mess of growing up? I mean, he's going to get hooked, and after a while he'll want to marry me. And then there'll be no choice but to tell him of my past. Is that fair?"

"OK, Judy, let's look at it this way. First, you don't know what *his* past has been like, and second, I doubt that your past is all that lurid."

"What do you mean? The kids at the academy didn't know why I quit. I said I was going to Europe. Before I was 17, I was pregnant, married, divorced, had my baby, and gave it away—in that order. And since then, things haven't been so innocent, either. My friends and I made the drug scene frequently, and not as spectators, either."

"Well, Judy, I still say you have no obligation to wear a placard telling the world of your indiscretions. Jesus is willing to forgive and to cast your sins in the depths of the sea. If Joe is a real Christian, he'll be more concerned about where you're going than where you've been. If his interest continues, I think you should tell him when he suggests marriage. Then it's up to him."

As school drew to a close, I noticed Judy and Joe together more and more, always radiant. They identified with campus religious programs in a joyful spirit. By graduation day she was wearing his pin. Upon returning to my office after spending the summer abroad, I found a letter from Judy, bearing her married name. In it she explained that before accepting Joe's proposal for marriage she had told him of her past, and he assured her that his love could overlook that. He also assured her that he had no such history, to her great relief. Her letter exuded a double joy—that of a happy bride and a happy Christian.

Joe was drafted, and while waiting to join him, Judy stopped in at the college. Her conversation was totally free of any self-doubt or guilt. Apparently she had taken her Saviour at His word and accepted His forgiveness completely. And having done that, she felt secure in Joe's Christlike willingness to forget that phase of her life. Our discussion was all about the present and the future.

When Joe's military service was nearly complete, I received a recommendation form from the General Conference—Judy and Joe were being considered for a mission appointment.

Not every young person can accept Christ's forgiveness so completely. Unfortunately, most cannot forgive themselves, and always feel contaminated by their past. In fact, I am impressed that one of the most difficult tasks that a pastoral counselor faces is helping an individual really accept the fact that when Christ forgives, He makes him a new person.

CHAPTER 16

SICK? OR JUST IRRESPONSIBLE?

When a student allows the Spirit to take control of his life, it's beautiful. When he seeks other solutions to his problems, he's headed for trouble. Judy's mixed-up life straightened out beautifully; the Lord was willing to work for Dort, too.

Southeast Asia Union College in Singapore draws students from several nearby countries, as well as from the island republic of Singapore. Dort was from one of these outlying regions.

When we first connected with the college, Dort was teaching in a secondary school in the neighboring mission, having finished an A.S. degree. According to reports, he was doing a good job teaching physical education and some science classes. PE seemed to be the field in which he excelled, for he was blessed with a near-perfect physique and kept himself in top condition.

When we received an application expressing his desire to return for the upper biennium, we accepted him. Rumor had it that Dort's girlfriend had bounced him and that he was badly shaken up, but when he moved into our dorm, he seemed to fit in well except for an occasional complaint about his temper having a short fuse. My observation was that he was handsome, athletic, and well read.

Occasionally students would comment on his odd behavior. He not only enjoyed shocking people; he seemed to want to draw attention to his broken heart. Someone suggested that he talk to a psychologist at Woodbridge, Singapore's very modern, well-staffed mental hospital, located not far from our college. The psychologist there felt that Dort had the potential for mental illness, so recommended a few days in the hospital for observation. My wife and I visited him on Sabbath, and everything seemed to be fine. Except for the locked doors, the facilities were better than those at our dormitory.

Later we learned that Dort had become violent, and would be undergoing shock therapy. He had moved back to our dorm, and when I asked him about the episode I'd heard about, he said merely that while he was in the ward an attendant had roughed up a patient, so he, Dort, lost his cool and broke a chair over the attendant's head.

"The guy deserved it," he said, "and I was merely righting a wrong the other patients were afraid to deal with. However, the psychologist then took me to the head psychiatrist, Dr. Teng, who changed my diagnosis from schizo-affective to something more serious. They've given me two electric shock treatments, but I'm not having any more of that."

"Dort, has it occurred to you that perhaps you're not really sick?"

"What do you mean, I'm not sick? The psychiatrist has diagnosed me as definitely schizoid. They're hoping to find a cure, and then I'll be OK."

"You're not going to like to hear this, but I don't think you're sick. The doctors have given you a label that excuses your irresponsibility. As long as you feel you're mentally ill, you cannot be held responsible for bizarre behavior, so you have no incentive to self-control. It is time you took over the management of your own life."

Although Dort was defensive, he was not particularly resentful of my attitude. We talked at length a number of times, and I always pressed him to quit relying on medicine and to exercise his God-given will. I lent him a reputable book on the subject, referred him to pertinent scriptures, and prayed with him that God would be allowed to lead in his life.

Early one morning he phoned, stating that he had a big problem. When I asked what it was, he said, "Well, Dr. Aaen, I didn't take my tranquilizer last night, and I lay awake thinking about something one of the boys said to me, and the more I thought about it, the madder I got. Finally, about midnight I got up and went to the guy's room and beat him up in his bed. Really, I'm a sick man!"

"OK, I'll buy that, Dort. You're sick. And since we do not run a medical institution, you just pack your things and get yourself over to Woodbridge. Under no circumstances are you to spend another night in our dorm."

"But Dr. Aaen, you can't punish me for being sick. I can't help what I do."

"Let's say we are not punishing you, but are just placing you where you can get the care a mentally sick person needs. Also, we are protecting the other fellows from a supposed pathological mental case. You get out to Woodbridge right away and tell the doctors what has happened. And remember, the dorm is off limits to you. This is for your protection, too. I know your dormmates, and they'll take steps to protect themselves. It may not be too healthy there for you. Better be gone before they take things into their own hands."

Sure enough, the boys in the dorm were quite irate, and the talk was less than tolerant. Dort would have been as welcome there that night as a mongoose in a den of cobras. After lunch I received a phone call from Dr. Teng at Woodbridge, explaining that Dort had slipped into a more serious category, displaying homicidal tendencies. Apparently Dort had convinced the good psychiatrist that he was a very sick boy. I sympathized, and suggested they keep him at the hospital till things at the college simmered down. Further, I explained that we had no facilities to care for one with such an illness, so we could not be responsible for him in the dorm.

About a week later the doctor phoned again, saying that they had found the right medication and that Dort was now all right. Would we take him back into the dormitory? No, thanks. He had claimed his previous outbreak had resulted from failure to take his tranquilizer, and since we had no control over his medicine, and indeed wanted no such responsibility, we could not allow him back in the dorm. He could attend classes, but must find other lodging.

Although less than ecstatic about the prohibition, Dort came back to classes. For some inexplicable reason he wore his mental-illness label like a badge of distinction. At the drop of a hint, he would tell about the horror of electric shock therapy, and how he put fear into the hospital attendants.

One afternoon Debbie Sung, an attractive secondary-school girl who lived in the college dorm, dropped by my office. Soon she was explaining about poor Dort, who had been confiding in her about how unfairly he was being treated by not being allowed to stay in the dormitory. Since Dort was not above using this sweet little thing to further his cause, I decided to send the weapon back to his camp.

"Debbie, I don't want you, under any circumstances, to be alone with Dort. He brags that he's a man of strong passions. He says he's not responsible for what happens when people cross him. He has displayed violence, as you well know. Now, you're an attractive young woman, and he has normal male impulses. The difference between him and the other fellows is that he claims he cannot control himself, while other guys feel obligated to behave themselves. Have you noticed how muscular he is? So, just don't ever meet him outside a group."

She was properly shaken.

"Do you think he'd commit rape?"

"I don't know what he'd do, and neither does he. Some rape victims are killed because, in panic, the rapist wants to quiet the only witness. Don't play with danger."

When she left my office, I sat back and waited. Predictably, within an hour or so, Dort arrived, quite upset.

"What have you told Debbie Sung about me? What do you think I am, a dog?"

"No, Dort, you're not a dog; you're an unguided missile. By your own words you are a man of strong passions, a powerful body with no recognized controls. You cannot stand to be crossed. Now you develop an interest in one of our most provocative girls, who is innocent and unlearned in the ways of the world. Her mother expects the school to protect her, and I aim to do so. What I told her, I'll tell you: No dates with her—or any of our other girls. Dort, you are being judged out of your own mouth, plus the statements of your psychiatrist and psychologist."

"Don't you think I have a conscience?"

"What kind of conscience permits a man to sneak

into another fellow's room and beat him senseless when he's sleeping and can't defend himself?"

"But I'm sick. Dr. Teng told you that."

"OK, OK, but you can't have it both ways. If you're mentally sick, you're not responsible. And as long as you are not responsible, stay out of our dorm and stay away from our girls. That's firm."

"But what if I promise never to lose control of myself again? How about that?"

"I'd say Amen. You'd be on the right track."

"OK, then can I move into the dorm, and date Debbie?"

"Maybe someday. Time alone will establish whether you're able to act responsibly, or, in reality, you have no control. For the time being, we want to see you prove yourself. Remember, I have always contended that you are not mentally ill, but are using mental illness as an excuse to act irresponsibly. You show us a period of responsible behavior, and we'll lift the restrictions. But not right away. I am taking no chances with the safety of our students."

Poor Dort! He had worked himself into a corner. Either he could abandon his "mentally ill, therefore not responsible" position and accept the usual restraints of society, or continue to claim to be sick and voluntarily isolate himself from associations that he really wanted. He saw that he couldn't have it both ways. Before he left the office I prayed that the Lord would give him strength to become mature, to exercise his divinely bestowed will.

Late that same afternoon Dr. Teng called. To my surprise, he was chuckling.

"Dort has just left my office, after informing me that we don't know what we're doing, that we've been contributing to his problem rather than relieving it."

"I'm sorry to hear that, Dr. Teng. He should be more respectful."

"Wait, Dr. Aaen. You haven't heard the whole story. He says that *you* have the solution to his problem, and that we have encouraged him to act irrationally. He's determined to exercise strong self-control and prove that he is *not* sick. I and my colleagues will be very interested in watching Dort for the next few weeks. Since one of our psychologists attends your church, we can keep an eye on Dort, even if he does not come to Woodbridge for consultation. We indeed may have been too quick to make excuses for him, giving a medical explanation for irresponsible behavior. I hope your solution will succeed, since so far he has not really profited from our treatment."

I thanked him, and then thanked God. I should add that had Dort been willing early on to submit his will to the leading of the Holy Spirit, he never would have gone to Woodbridge in the first place. Somehow I could not get him to make that surrender.

It would be fine to report that all of Dort's troubles ended at that point. This was not the case, but I *can* say that we never knew of him losing his temper again. He was not entirely happy that we denied him access to the dorm for the rest of the year—there was a backlog of hostility among the boys that needed time to cool. He became accepted among his peers in time, and even took positions of leadership in student activities.

The last I heard of Dort, he was again teaching in one of our secondary schools. Dort's previous conduct had been such that when his former girlfriend got married, the wedding was not publicized for fear of violence on his part. They need not have worried; Dort was now a different person.

CHAPTER 17

UNSCHEDULED ENCOUNTER

When dealing with a fellow like Dort, a counselor wishes for some shortcut to strip away the self-delusions that keep people from seeing themselves clearly. Our Lord had such skill.

It was noon. Having walked fifteen or twenty miles since morning, Jesus and His disciples, en route from Judea to Galilee via a shortcut across Samaria, stopped for rest and refreshment at Jacob's well, about a ten-minute walk from the village of Sychar. Obviously there were no roadside diners or ice-cream stands, so the disciples went on to the village to buy some food. Even though they had arrived at the famous well, its cool waters were not readily available to them, since they had neither rope nor vessel. And at noon very few villagers would be drawing water from its hundred-foot depths—they customarily came in the cool of the mornings and evenings.

The Biblical account, found in John 4, states simply that Jesus was weary and that He sat down, presumably on the ledge beside the well, awaiting the return of His friends with nourishment, and hopefully the arrival of a villager with equipment for drawing water. I can imagine His interest as the solitary Samaritan woman approached and went about letting her jug down to the cool depths, the splashing and gurgling as it filled, and the dripping with hollow echoes as it was pulled up.

Cordiality was definitely not the order of the day between the Jews and Samaritans, so I can picture the studied unconcern of the woman as she hoisted her jug onto the ledge, quite aware of being watched by the weary Stranger. She was not offended by His silence; the last thing she had in mind was a counseling interview. Jesus, on the other hand, considered every contact to be a witnessing opportunity, every individual a candidate for eternal life. To her indifference He responded with a request. He knew that she would misunderstand, and perhaps rebuff, a simple greeting. But He also knew the Oriental culture, in which no request for help could be denied. Moreover, since water was life, a request for it would assuredly be granted. So He simply asked for a drink.

There are counselors who feel that they have no right to intrude or to intervene in anyone's life. I agree that a counselor can accomplish nothing if his services are not welcome. But notice how Jesus made an opening with this woman of Sychar. He was totally nonthreatening. He merely broke through the barrier of centuries of mutual distrust. He was not afraid to violate a cultural taboo, and that really shocked the woman.

I never fail to marvel at Jesus' ability to vary His approach according to the dynamics of the situation and the needs of the individual. However, there is one principle that can be applied in a general way to all situations: Never fail to be friendly and open, no matter whether the individual appears to want friendship or not. I recall once when a young woman came to my office for some information on an assignment. She was accompanied by another girl, whom I didn't know. As they left, the friend, who hadn't said a word, seemed to hesitate just a second. Without thinking, I addressed her casually, asking, "How is everything going with you?"

Without hesitation she answered, "Terrible, just awful. But who on this campus can I talk to?"

I assured her I would be happy to discuss her problems with her, and she dropped into the chair as though she had been pushed there. Her friend left, and I rather wondered if the whole thing had been staged to put the troubled one into a situation where she could get help. At this time I haven't the foggiest recollection of what her problem was, but I do remember that it was important to her.

As I see it, Jesus took a certain risk in opening a conversation with the woman at Jacob's well. As He showed later, He knew what kind of woman she was. In a small town like Sychar, everyone must have known her well. What if someone came by and found Him chatting with a five-time-married woman who had apparently given up all such formality and just moved in with number six? But then, Jesus never drew back from association with any sinner for fear of besmirching His own good name.

Some time ago I was talking to a Christian friend who teaches medicine at Loma Linda. He explained that he was on his way to Chicago for a reunion of his high school graduating class. Further, the reunion was to be on a Sabbath afternoon. Perhaps I registered surprise, or was expected to, for the doctor said, "I haven't seen those classmates of mine in years. They don't know what the Lord has done in my life, and I feel compelled to go and tell them. I have no illusions about the atmosphere—lots of alcohol and smoking and cheap music and dancing—

but I'm going to witness, not for entertainment."

Even so, Jesus, whose title as Counselor had been established hundreds of years before His birth, was concerned only with implanting truth in the mind of this chance acquaintance at the well in Samaria. Chance acquaintance? Hardly. To those led of God, there are no chance occurrences. But I digress.

Too surprised to reflect, the woman says in essence, "Hey, how come *you* are asking *me* for a drink? Jews and Gentiles just don't do these things!"

Any speech teacher can tell you that the first objective of a speaker is to get attention. I recall one humorous lecturer who walked onto the platform, pulled a pistol from under his coat, and fired two or three blanks toward the ceiling. "Now that I have your attention," he said, "we can go on with the talk." Jesus used surprise to get the attention and break the ice, for unlike Nicodemus, who sought Him out, this woman probably didn't expect to hear or speak a word with this cultural Pariah.

Then, having engaged her in conversation, He wasted no time on small talk, but challenged her curiosity by saying that if she knew who was asking her for a drink, she would be asking living water of *Him*. Cool as the water was from the depths of Jacob's well, it lacked the sweetness of that which gushed from some of the springs on the side of Mount Gerizim. This water was often spoken of as "living water," in contrast to well water.

Again, He had her on the end of a string of curiosity. She couldn't see any waterpot, and He didn't even have a rope for the well. How could He give her water? She reminded Him that Jacob had worked hard to dig this well for the benefit of his household, his cattle, and succeeding generations.

Gradually bringing her from the here and now to universal verities of eternal importance, He made another startling statement: "If you drink from this well, you will need more water in a few hours. But I've got better water. With it you'll never thirst—it will stay with you and give you eternal life." Now He had accomplished step number two, creating a desire for what He had to offer. Note that He was constantly leading, never pushing.

Thinking of all those tiresome trips from home to the well and back, she said, "Give me this wonderful water so I don't get thirsty, and don't have to come out here all the time with this miserable jug!"

From indifference to eagerness in a few deft moves! This is counseling in the finest sense. Now for the next step: decision—or, if you prefer, behavior modification.

If Jesus was human enough to be tired and hungry, He was doubtlessly human enough to enjoy her reaction when He said, "All right. Go get your husband, and come back."

That was simple enough. He couldn't possibly know, the women thought, what a shambles she had made of her domestic affairs. She was a quick thinker, so without lying she reported, "I have no husband." He certainly couldn't tell by looking at her whether that meant she was widowed, divorced, or had never married. Clever answer, she thought.

Counselors usually have to work with whatever information the counselee gives them. Only occasionally do they have other sources that provide them insights that the counselee does not realize they have.

Such as the time when Lenie was defending herself by trying to make me feel guilty when I suggested she was getting into bad company.

"You're just looking for an excuse to kick me out of school. Why don't you pick on someone else for a change!"

"Lenie, that's simply not true. You don't know who your real friends are. I want to help you, but you won't allow me to be your friend."

"I do too know who my friends are, and you certainly are not one of them! You just want to make trouble for me so you can expel me."

"OK, Lenie, do you think the two fellows with whom you spent last Saturday night at the beach are your friends? If so, then how come I know about it? And if I'm such an enemy, why didn't I bring this to the discipline committee and have you expelled on Monday?"

"Whatever those guys said about me is a lie! I didn't want to go out there, and I demanded they bring me back, but they refused. The buses don't run that late, and I could hardly walk ten miles in high heels."

And the tears flowed freely. It isn't often that I have such inside information before a counseling session (if this confrontation could be called counseling). However, it gave Lenie some insights as to whom to trust, and paved the way for subsequent, more fruitful encounters.

The woman's clever answer exploded in her face when Jesus said, "You're quite right in saying you have no husband, since you've had five husbands, and the man you now have is not your husband. You told the truth, all right."

The neighbors may have been aware of her lurid love life, but certainly there was no way this itinerant Jew could have known. It's possible that she had committed her indiscretions long ago and far away, and that her current friends didn't even know her true marital status. In any case, it was obvious that this man had supernatural sources of data. All she could say in the face of such miraculous mind reading was "I know you're a prophet!"

As have counselees the world over, she saw an urgent need to move the topic away from embarrassing personal revelations. Flattery might be effective. And if this man was a prophet, why not settle a question that the Jews and Samaritans had been haggling over ever since the time of Ezra—was it proper to worship at the Samaritan center here on Mount Gerizim (although the temple was destroyed more than a hundred years earlier, they still had the altar), or must one worship only in Jerusalem?

Here again, Jesus led her away from minutiae and to eternal principles. Specifically, He pointed out that *where* one worshiped was not nearly as important as *how* one worshiped. Apparently this sounded a bit heavy theologically, and her brain was already reeling from this amazing interview, so she said, "Well, anyway, when the Messiah comes, He will explain all these things."

At this point the Saviour chose to make Himself known to this unsophisticated woman in a way He hadn't even used to His own disciples or to any of the Jews. All were looking for the Messiah, and some had speculated that He might be Jesus of Nazareth, but this was the Lord's first emphatic avowal of which we have record.

"I that speak to you am He."

About this time the disciples returned with food, and the interview ended. The Bible says she left her waterpot at the well and went into Sychar. Either she was so excited she forgot it or she wanted no cumbersome jug to slow her down.

In this brief encounter, we see the Master Counselor get the attention of an indifferent stranger, create in her a desire for something better, bring her to a conviction, or decision, and then watch that conviction become action as she hastens to town and brings Him an audience that holds Him for two days of preaching and answering questions.

It is interesting to observe the woman's method of stirring interest among her fellow townsmen. She didn't say, "I have found the Messiah." Rather, she piqued their curiosity by a bit of exaggeration, stating that He told her everything she ever did, and then raising the question "Can this be the Christ?"

Apparently her credibility was not exactly impeccable, for later they told her they accepted Him as the Saviour of the world, not because of her word, but because they had heard Him themselves.

An interesting footnote to this episode was made by the Lord Himself as He and His disciples left Sychar after an exhilarating two days of preaching and teaching an eager and receptive audience of Samaritans. Resuming the interrupted journey from Judea to His Galilean homeland, and savoring the sweet memory of warmth and acceptance, He made the famous statement "A prophet has no honor in his own country." Sad, but all too true. Human nature seems to concur that "an expert is a man from out of town."

CHAPTER 18

A MATTER OF SELF-IMAGE

The woman at the well may not have been the smartest citizen of Sychar, but she had the virtue of being willing to recognize and accept help when it came to her. Not all counselees will do that. Consider Tyrone.

Teaching the honors section of Freshman Composition is fun. Class discussions are lively, and the themes are seldom disappointing; the teacher can deal primarily with content, since these students can handle the form and technique quite well. Assignments tend to be on time.

However, one of my sharpest boys, from the standpoint of class participation, failed to hand in the first two or three themes, so I called him in and asked him what the problem was.

"I always have trouble getting homework in. I just goof off. Frankly, those assignments are kid stuff; I could have done them in the ninth grade."

"OK, Tyrone, but how do *I* know you can do them? The only way I can grade you is by the work you turn in. We assume that you expect to meet course requirements when you register. How else do you expect to get a grade?"

"Oh, I'll probably flunk. That's my pattern. I could easily be a four-point student, but I never get the work in, so I fail."

"What makes you think you could get A's so easily?"

"I cool any test I take; that's how I got into Honors English class. I'll bet I had the top score on the placement test. I'm a genius."

"And so modest! Who told you that you are a genius?"

"Why should I be modest? I know what I can do. I've taken IQ tests and all that stuff since grade school. Everybody has always told me I was smart. I'll tell you something else—I'm good-looking, too. I can have any girl I want (although I'm really no good), and they know it. They can't resist me."

"What do you mean, you're no good?"

"Look, this isn't the first college I've been to. Last year I was kicked out of one. It was just as well, I suppose; I was headed for F's in everything—too many absences and no homework."

"I'm curious. Would you mind telling me why you were expelled?"

"Well, you see, I talked myself into a job in the city nearby as an emcee of a television talk show on Sabbath afternoons. It went along fine—great viewer ratings—until someone out at the college turned on his TV set when he shouldn't have. I'll wash out here, too. I'm really a gold-plated phony. So you see why I say I'm no good. I know myself. I drive the psychiatrists crazy because I talk their language and anticipate their diagnosis and counsel."

"Then you've had psychiatric care? Who sent you to them?"

"My old man is a doctor, and my mother has a Ph.D. in psychology, but they never could manage me. So they handed me over to the shrinks. That was a laugh; I made monkeys out of several of them. If I had all the bread my folks have spent on psychiatrists for me, I could retire."

"I notice you're going with Sheri. What's she doing with a self-confessed gold-plated phony?"

"That's *her* problem. Her folks know my folks, so they should know I'm no good for her, but I just turn on the charm when we go to their place, and they think I'm great. I've told Sheri not to fall for me, but she won't listen—just like the others."

"Sounds like you're out to break your parents' hearts. Don't you care whether you hurt them?"

"It's true that I embarrass them—they've got their professional reputations to think about, you know. But I've never really felt that they love me an awful lot. They probably didn't want me in the first place, so why should I worry about them?"

That was probably the most unsatisfactory encounter that ever took place in my office. I felt helpless, frustrated, and sad. This boy had all the factors for failure solidly lined up—too much money, too much brains, too handsome, no conscience, no humility, a confirmed cynicism, and no respect for his parents. And he plainly wanted no help from me or anyone else.

As he predicted, his stay on our campus was less than one quarter. Although I wanted to call Sheri and warn her, it hardly seemed a gesture that would be appreciated or effective. She did break with him before he left, but for what reason I never learned.

The Greeks centered their dramas on what they called a tragic flaw. What was Tyrone's tragic flaw? (Certainly he was a tragic figure, if I ever met one!) To point up what I think his problem was, let me recount another experience, this time on the other side of the world.

My wife and I were active in the information and

education program of the Singapore Family Planning Association for a number of years. That was our "extracurricular activity." For the most part, we participated in Preparation for Marriage seminars in YMCAs, churches, youth hostels, and schools. When an international conference of the IPPF (International Planned Parenthood Federation) was held in Penang, I was sent as a delegate. The week went rapidly, with papers presented by experts from many nations, and lively discussions to keep one awake.

One delegate made a speech stating that since the youth of the world are caught up in what he termed the sexual revolution, and no one waits for marriage, all we can do to avoid overpopulation is provide them with plenty of information and contraceptive paraphernalia. When he sat down, I asked for the floor and identified myself as a Christian educator and minister. Essentially, I said something like this:

"To assume cynically that all youth are selfish hedonists is to ignore the facts. Today we find youth willing to die for a variety of causes they think are important, from pacifism to ecology. We must capitalize on their intrinsic idealism—sell them on the dangers of overpopulation, and the world's need for people who will act responsibly. Tell them that the standards of their forefathers were good standards, good for the individual, the family, and society. I refuse to believe that the youth of this generation are interested only in gratifying their own wants. Let's promote responsibility."

What impression, if any, my sermonette had on the assembled delegates, I have no way of knowing. However, after that meeting, three young women stopped me and asked to talk. They were students at the local university, sent as observers to the IPPF meetings, to report back to their sociology class. One girl spoke for the group:

"We want to thank you for putting in a word in defense of us. What on earth does that guy think we are—a bunch of prostitutes? We resent the implication that we have no morals. We're virgins and we will be virgins till we're properly married. Most of our friends also live by conventional standards of morality, as far as we know. Thanks for speaking for us."

We had a good visit, during which I found that one girl was a Buddhist, one a Moslem, and the third professed no religion. All three were attractive, intelligent young moderns. Being by nature a curious person, I asked whether I might question them further. Permission was cheerfully granted.

"I'd like to know the basis of your moral standards. We Christians take the Ten Commandments as a guide. Since you represent diverse religious views, let me ask whether your religion sets your moral guidelines."

They thought awhile, talked among themselves, and decided that it was not religious tenets that set their behavioral patterns. So I took another approach.

"Did your parents—one or both—explain the birds and the bees and lay down rules for your relations with the fellows?"

They laughed hilariously at that. Apparently sex was pretty much a taboo topic in their homes. Their no-nos were not parental edicts. Then where did they get their code of morals? Were the men they associated with simply above that sort of thing, removing both temptation and opportunity? Definitely not. In fact, they felt that the young men kept them altogether under too much pressure. Then what was the secret? Some interesting dynamics were operating here, for sure.

At this point there was a lot of animated conversation among them, most of which was in English, and fortunately what was in Malay, I could understand too. They finally settled it, though it seemed that none of them had given the matter enough thought to clarify it before.

"We have always known what was acceptable conduct for ladies. Our society frowns on promiscuous girls. We also love our parents, and are proud of our families. What hurts one of us hurts all. So we are not about to let them down."

That visit with three fine young women of another culture summarized a truth I have observed often on both sides of the Pacific—one of the strongest constraints, or restraints, on human behavior is what the family, or, as the psychologists say, "significant others," expect of us. But this force is effective only if there is mutual love and respect. Tyrone did not respect his parents, so their influence on him was minimal. My wife used to be a probation officer in the juvenile court, where she often saw teen-agers deliberately get themselves into big trouble just to lash out at parents who would not pay attention to them otherwise. When the kid spoke, his parents were too busy or too indifferent to listen, but when the juvenile authorities phoned, they became aware of their offspring.

Another instance comes to mind—with a happier ending than the one to Tyrone's story. Pam returned to campus from a weekend at home and, as she occasionally did, stopped in my office for a report of the trip. Home wasn't the coziest place for her—her dad was an alcoholic, and her mom led a questionable social life—so Pam spent part of the weekend with her sister and brother-in-law.

"On Sunday morning my brother-in-law worked

on my car for a while, and then suggested that we take a drive to check it out. When he stopped along a secluded road I realized he really wanted to check *me* out! I haven't had boyfriends and I guess I was just too naive, but suddenly I realized I was getting involved in something I had no business in. But he was determined. It's awful to say, but I almost made the biggest mistake of my life."

"Pam, I'm curious. What made you wake up and reverse the action?"

"It's silly, I suppose, but I suddenly thought, What would Elder Aaen think! I know you have confidence in me, and I'm not about to let you down."

What a pity that she couldn't have said, like Joseph, "How can I sin against God?" or "I must not disappoint Mom and Dad," or even "Hey, I'm not that kind of girl!"

On the other hand, it's a sobering thought to a minister or teacher or counselor to know that his belief or confidence in a student may be the major restraint upon that student when temptations come on strong.

Ideally, a person should have such a strong self-respect that nothing can shake him. Joseph did not tell Potiphar's wife, "I'm not that kind of man!" Rather, he emphatically stated his allegiance to God and his determination not to disappoint Him. Poor Tyrone—no self-respect, no filial respect, no respect for his Creator. Therefore, no control.

CHAPTER 19

DOES GOD READ THE DATE?

Some young people, like Tyrone, deliberately flaunt unconventionality. Some try to abide by society's mores, but find themselves in conflict with custom anyway. And strangely, a clear-cut definition is not always easy to come by.

Someone once asked, "Does God read the date on the marriage license?" Good question.

Promiscuous or experimental sex is quite explicitly condemned in the Scriptures, so the counselor should have little difficulty in discussing it with young folks.

Trial marriages are un-Biblical too. But occasionally one faces a situation that falls outside the clearcut boundaries of the seventh commandment.

Take, for instance, the case of Oni, our household servant some years ago in Java. One morning she showed up for work very agitated. So I inquired what was distressing her.

"Elder Aaen, will you baptize me today? I just don't want to wait a bit longer. Today, *please!*"

"Wait a minute. What's all the hurry? You're not quite through the Bible studies with Elder Mamora. If he feels you are ready when he completes the series, we will be happy to baptize you. That should be in a couple weeks. OK?"

Our college was built in a Moslem area, not because we deliberately chose such an environment, but because land was available there and it was only twelve miles from union headquarters. Consequently it was a live-in situation for students, and the staff was provided homes on the campus. There were no Christian neighbors close by. With most of the teachers' wives needed to teach classes, it was necessary to employ domestic help in the homes, and we had hired Oni, a woman who lived in the next kampong, or village. We quickly developed a real fondness for her ready smile and quiet efficiency. Until his death in a train accident, her husband had divided his time between her and her two sons and another wife about fifty miles to the north. This cozy arrangement is quite acceptable to Moslems, and whatever tensions Oni felt she kept to herself.

When we were forced to expel one of our less-than-zealous Christians, whom I shall call William, he elected to take a job in a nearby military post rather than return to his home island. In fact, he settled in Oni's kampong and began courting the young widow. Since it is forbidden in Indonesia for a Moslem to marry a Christian, when William and Oni asked the local guru agama (religious teacher) to arrange their marriage, William was asked if he would become a Moslem. He assured the guru that he would come for studies in the Koran soon, and for a fee the guru presented them with a paper indicating that they were husband and wife. However, William apparently had no intention of becoming a Moslem—religion was just not his thing.

When Bible studies began in the military post opposite Oni's kampong, she asked whether she might join, and of course Elder Mamora was glad to receive her into the group. It should be explained that most of the soldiers on that post came from Manado, a predominantly Christian area on the island of Sulawesi. It would have been difficult, if not impossible, to have held evangelistic meetings or Bible lessons at that time in any of the kampongs, totally Moslem as they were. In fact, when the word got out that Oni was studying to become a Christian, the citizens of the village above hers cut off the water to her village. This act, rather than forcing her neighbors to pressure her to change her mind, made them so angry that they rallied behind Oni, and appealed to higher authorities to have the stream reopened, which was done within hours. One has to live in that area to realize the importance of the stream to each kampong—it provides the domestic water supply, irrigation of crops and fishponds, and community sewer.

But back to Oni. When she practically demanded immediate baptism, I asked her to wait. I wanted to know the reason for the sudden rush to the baptistry.

"Well, you know when William and I were married a couple months ago, the guru agama gave us a paper, and we gave him 200 rupiahs. Last evening he came to my home and asked to see the paper, so we got it out and showed it to him. He simply tore it to bits, and handed back our 200 rupiahs, saying that we were now divorced. I guess he was angry because William never went to study the Koran, and now he has heard that I am studying the Bible. I must quickly become a Christian so we can be married. Today if possible."

"Hold on, Oni. Isn't your marriage registered at the camat's office? The guru agama had to do that."

"That's what I told him, but he says he decided not to register the marriage until William became a Moslem. So there's no record. We are not married."

"Well, Oni, I don't consider this sufficient basis for a hasty baptism. Just be patient for two or three weeks and you can doubtless be baptized with the others studying in Elder Mamora's class."

"Yes, but what am I to do with William in the meantime? I don't want to send him away, and he doesn't want to go. Are we living in sin?"

"All right, Oni, do you consider before God that you are married to William?"

"Of course. And William considers me his wife."

"And do you think God is worried about the paper the guru tore up?"

"No. That man is not working for God. What does God care about what he does with that paper?"

"Then why should you send William away? You have done your best to follow the prescriptions of God and society. Now, as soon as you are baptized, we will formalize the marriage. The important thing is your fidelity to your marriage vows."

And that's what was done. In due time I had the thrill of baptizing her—the first Moslem in that area to accept Jesus Christ. Although William was a Christian only in the loosest application of the term, he had been baptized earlier, so their marriage was acceptable to the government and to society.

The danger here is in extrapolating from this isolated case a conclusion that is not warranted. Sooner or later every counselor meets an engaged couple who argue that, since they are totally committed to each other, they are for all practical purposes married. *Ergo*, why wait for the intimacies until the big ceremony?

All right, let's look at that thought for a moment. What is the purpose of the engagement? Basically, it is a period of testing the relationship, a time of tentative commitment, when either party can honorably cancel out. No matter how "married" the two principals may consider themselves, in the eyes of society they are not joined, and a change of mind by one or the other is acceptable.

Further, the secrecy and furtiveness of conduct not approved by society hardly seems the best way to initiate the marriage bed. And would not the marriage night and the honeymoon seem sort of an anticlimax? Not long ago a young divorcee told me that she and her husband had "ruined" their honeymoon by previously living together.

Another variation of this theme is illustrated by the experience of a couple we will call Bill and Bonnie. They were madly in love, but were only sophomores in college. Before their junior year, they went to talk to Bill's folks, suggesting that two can live as cheaply as one, and asking what the folks would think if they got married just before school started, instead of the following summer as they had planned. His folks expressed limited enthusiasm for that scheme and advised them to wait a year. One objection they mentioned was the possibility of an unwanted pregnancy. Bill's confident answer was that they were not worried about that, since they had "read a good book on the subject."

As Bill and Bonnie drove back to the college, they both expressed disappointment and resentment at the folks' lack of understanding, and one of them came up with an idea that would win no prize for originality—why not be married secretly, and then have the big wedding after school was out in the spring! No one need know. Maybe they'd tell the folks after the church ceremony, and everybody could have a big laugh.

The next State had no waiting period, so they drove directly to an isolated county seat whose newspaper was not likely to catch the attention of family or friends, and said their vows before strangers, paid their few dollars, and went on their way rejoicing. What a bargain! What a secret!

Within a week of registration Bonnie decided to take a job and an apartment near the college, and drop classes. The rest of us were surprised, but she explained that her mother could not send any more money for tuition, as she had been doing the past two years. Within a couple months Bill was in trouble with the dean for spending too many evenings in her apartment. The neighbors were talking.

Shortly after Thanksgiving, Bill informed me, rather sheepishly, that he was dropping out of school. When I asked how come, he explained that he and Bonnie had gotten married in September, and that she was now pregnant. At least he didn't have to go apartment hunting! Their friends were invited over for meals, and facing the front door was a framed marriage certificate. Not much was said, but the purpose was clear. An interesting postscript is that when they wrote and told his folks how their scheme had backfired, Bill's mother answered that they must have read the same book she and his father had read. Did that framed marriage certificate in their front room silence all gossip? I doubt it.

So what's wrong with a secret marriage? Simply that the couple is living a lie. When the Lord says in the second chapter of Genesis that a man shall leave his parents and join his wife, that implies a public declaration, and a genuine joining—not a secretive, clandestine liaison that fears disclosure.

While it is ridiculous to say that God reads the date on the marriage license, He certainly reads hearts. Marriage is both a public and a private matter.

Are there no exceptions to this rule? Is no one

married who does not have a public—and preferably a church—wedding? The answer to that is fairly clear, but like all rules, it has its exceptions. Years ago one of our pastors went to the island of Timor, and the Lord blessed his efforts with many baptisms. When his reports to the union began to show almost as many marriages as baptisms, the president wrote him a letter asking what was behind all the weddings, sometimes more than one a day.

The good minister answered that in the past the local custom made no provision for a marriage ceremony, and until recently the government kept no record of such formalities. Therefore, he felt that all his parishioners, be they grandparents or parents, were living in sin! He was correcting the situation as fast as he could. Needless to say, he was informed that he should cease imposing a ceremony on good souls whose loyalty and devotion to their partners was beyond question.

There are still other situations to challenge the pastor or counselor. A colleague of mine was a missionary in a country that granted no divorce, period. The result of that rigidity was a plethora of common-law marriages, some estimates running as high as 40 to 50 percent of all families. An engaged couple graduated from our college on a bright Sunday morning. After the graduation exercises were over, there was a two- or three-hour period before the girl was to board ship for her home island. They planned to spend that short interval with another engaged couple, also newly graduated. The topic of marriage inevitably came up, and on an impulse the first couple decided to go to the marriage registry and be married quietly, before the ship sailed. There was just enough time to complete the formalities and get the girl on board the ship. A tearful farewell, and the new bride was off, with vague plans to return as soon as possible, probably in three or four months. The groom was entering graduate school immediately.

At first the letters were frequent and tender. Then he became immersed in his studies, and she began working at the job her family had arranged for her.

To shorten the narrative, the letters cooled, slowed, and stopped. The last letter she wrote said she had fallen in love with someone else.

In due time he found a fine Christian nurse, fell in love, and began talking of marriage. She could accept the debacle he had gotten into, and was willing to overlook it. At this point they came to my friend, the missionary. Would he marry them? Of course. But there was this little detail of the previous marriage, which was never consummated but was a matter of official record. This meant they could not legally marry; it would have to be a common-law marriage. That knowledge placed my friend in a dilemma: the government forbade remarriage of currently married people, so a church marriage was out. Then, what about a home wedding? Again, my friend had to decline, lest the church be accused of illegal activities.

So what can we conclude from all of this? First, a counselor must apply the principles of the Book, whether it is convenient or not. He must deal with each case on its own merits, for there will be an occasional unique situation.

Genesis 2:24—repeated by others (including the Saviour Himself) four times later in the Scriptures—tells us that marriage is both a public and a private matter. It is not a true marriage if one of those stipulations is not complied with. All of which should answer the question of premarital sex and secret marriages.

CHAPTER 20

SELF-DESTRUCTION: NO LAUGHING MATTER

As I think back on the students with whom I've talked, laughed, prayed, and wept, a variety of emotions washes over me. There were some very happy endings, and some not so happy—in fact, tragic. Like the young man who stopped at our home one afternoon to express his concern that his girlfriend was reluctant to talk seriously about the future. He feared she was rejecting him because of one defective eye, a blemish that I hardly noticed. My wife and I reminded him that the young lady on whom he had set his affections was only 17, four years younger than he, so naturally her concerns about marriage would not match his. Also, we tried to reassure him that his eye problem was not as serious a social handicap as he imagined it to be. We had prayer with him, and he went on his way, seemingly encouraged.

Just what happened after he left our home is not clear, but the next morning we were horrified to learn that he had jumped to his death from a highrise apartment building.

This strange and tragic act made me reflect on other students who had talked about self-destruction. I had always considered suicide threats to be attention-getting ploys, and therefore not a very serious matter. For instance, there was Wim, who was smitten with love for a cute little girl of his own tribe, who worked in our home in Java. She complained to my wife and me that he was constantly bothering her with his attentions. So I called him in and suggested that he bestow his favors elsewhere, as Rodi was too young to be interested. He was noncommittal. Obviously my suggestions made no great impact on him.

Later, Rodi came in to say that Wim had said that if she wouldn't marry him, he would kill himself, and she'd be guilty the rest of her life. Although I considered this tactic to be unfair in the extreme, I told her to tell the young man that what he did with his life was not her responsibility. The answer was No, finally, positively, and irrevocably. I also stated that she need have no fear that he would destroy himself, as he had shown himself to be a man of words rather than action.

Apparently she followed my instructions, probably with embellishments, for later Wim appeared in my office, quite hostile. "Did you advise Rodi to tell me to go ahead and kill myself?"

"No, I merely said it was no responsibility of hers as long as she was honest with you. I also told her not to worry, because you were obviously bluffing. Further, let me say that I think such a crude device as a suicide threat is a very low trick to force a girl into an unwanted marriage."

"Why don't you think it would be a good marriage? What's so bad about me? I'm talented. I speak better English than any student on the campus, and I sing and play the trumpet. What makes you think I'd be such a bad husband? I love Rodi."

"Wim, you're ten years older than Rodi. You've been expelled from two schools. You have a reputation on our campus for being more smoke than fire, and your grades make it doubtful that we can accept you next term. I agree that you have talent, but you'll need a year or so of consistent performance to prove that you have the most important quality for a good husband—character. Rodi is not interested in marriage now, since she's a long way from her educational goals."

Let's face it—I handled the matter poorly. Fortunately, I was right about Wim's not being serious in his suicide threat. Predictably, he never finished school, and has continued drifting from job to job, as he did earlier from school to school. Rodi finished the nursing course, married a European engineer, and traveled the world. My wife and I were entertained in their home in Paris one delightful day a few years later. However, if I had to deal with Wim again, I would not, either directly or indirectly, imply that he was a coward or that he was faking. Specialists agree that a great many suicides are never intended to be more than dramatic productions, to stop short of consummation when the desired effect has been achieved. However, often the timing goes wrong and death follows, unintentionally.

For instance, a girl we'll call Trudy was in my office to discuss a theme, which I found rambling and somewhat incoherent. However, no matter how I tried to direct the talk to rhetoric, she kept bringing up her pet topic—boys. Aware that this unkempt and unlovely young woman had deep-seated problems far beyond my competence to alleviate, I stood up and eased her out of my office, assuring her that if she ever needed help, she could always phone. The girls in the outer office laughed at my confusion, and told me that Trudy possessed quite a reputation as a predator, and was uniformly unsuccessful.

That evening I was telling my wife about this weird encounter, when the phone rang. It was Trudy.

"Do you remember how I looked this afternoon?"

"Well, yes, I guess I do. Why do you ask?"

"You better remember how I looked, 'cause you'll never see me again."

"And what does that mean?"

"Oh, I've just taken an overdose of medicine, so I won't be around long."

"Are you in your room?"

"Yes."

Some hasty phone calls to health service and the dean got things moving, but of course Trudy did not remain in her room. When she announced her impending demise to the desk monitor, that girl said, "I don't believe you; show me the bottle!" (I had already alerted her.) So Trudy waltzed up to her room and brought back the medication bottle. The monitor then called the doctor and read him the label. An ambulance was on the way, but when it got there Trudy was off to the cafeteria to spread the word. In due time the ambulance crew located her and took her to the hospital, where her stomach was pumped. She got the attention she wanted, poor girl, but the dormitory deans felt they could get along fine without her, so they shipped her home. We heard no more of Trudy, but it's entirely possible that a subsequent cry for attention was less successful.

Any dormitory dean with a few years' experience can give a version or two of the same old story. He doesn't take suicide talk lightly, and neither do I now. So if I had to deal with Wim again, I would not treat his case so casually.

As for the young man who jumped to his death,

there was no hint of self-destruction during his visit. Perhaps if I had been more perceptive I could have sensed desperation in his manner, but his action was a total surprise to all of us.

As a teacher of freshman English, I used to have my students buy a bound notebook of lined blank pages. Each Friday they were to hand in the notebooks, with a specified number of pages written on any topic they chose. We called it free writing. Needless to say, the reading of those assignments occupied a good portion of my Sundays.

One day as I was reading, a certain essay disturbed me. I read it again, and while there was nothing explicit, somehow a vague and disquieting cry for help seemed to come through, like the ring of a phone to a person taking a nap in an adjoining room. Although I had said I would not make public the contents of the free-writing booklets, I took this one to David Igler, at that time dean of the freshman men's dormitory, and asked him to read it. He had the same undefinable uneasy response that I did, suggesting that this boy might be suicidal. Later that afternoon he called to say that he had called the boy in for a visit and found that he indeed was planning to end his life, *that night!* Good counsel averted the tragedy, and as far as I know, the young man had a successful year. I never alluded to the matter, and doubtless he never knew how the dean sensed his crisis.

Suicide is from the darker side of the counseling work, but, like homosexuality, it's there, and must be faced. As in so many other counseling activities, sensitivity is the most useful tool in the counselor's kit, one that he should learn from his Saviour and cultivate assiduously.

CHAPTER 21

MOTIVATION: THERE'S NO TEST FOR IT

While the pastoral counselor may find most of his problems revolving around social matters, the teacher frequently confronts scholastic difficulties that have little to do with interpersonal relationships.

After reading dozens of freshman themes, an English teacher can spot a C paper from six feet away. Or at least he thinks he can. Jerry was by my standards a C student. His papers were uninspired, flawed with occasional misspellings, and plagued by poor punctuation. His only redeeming attribute was punctuality, both in attendance and assignments. Predictably, at the end of the fall quarter he got a C in Freshman Composition.

When the grades came out, Jerry appeared in my office with a very serious look on his face, saying, "Hey, you gave me a C, and I can't get any C's. I'm a premed student, and I have to have B's and A's."

This incongruity rather shocked me.

"Jerry, my friend, I gave you a C because you did average work."

"Yes, but I have to go to Loma Linda, and I can't get C's. What can I do to raise that grade?"

"Nothing. You did all the assignments, and they were all about the same. You were not absent from class, and there is no justification that I can give for changing the grade. So I am afraid it's going to have to stand."

"Yes, but that is not going to get me to Loma Linda. If I can't change that grade, what can I do for next quarter?"

"Well, Jerry, you might try a different teacher for English. As I think over your work for the past quarter, I am impressed with the fact that you did not proofread very well, and that you are not likely to wear out many dictionaries at the rate you are going. By the way, why are you so sure that you are going to Loma Linda?"

In my own thinking I had this boy classified as a very ordinary student whose goals were unrealistic. Young people whose parents are pushing them into professions for which they are not qualified, and perhaps to which they are not dedicated, are to be pitied. In my own heart I was convinced that Jerry, with his unrealistic aspirations, was headed for a disappointment, and that perhaps the earlier he faced up to the facts of life, the better.

"Mr. Aaen, I have always known that I was going to be a doctor. My father was a doctor. My uncles on both sides of the family were doctors. There is no other alternative for me."

"OK, Jerry, I understand clearly that you have a goal, but are you being realistic? The medical course is an extremely demanding one, and some students, even if they sincerely want to become physicians, are just not qualified. Have you considered something in the medical field other than the M.D. program?"

"No. And I'm not about to change my goals. I do not want to change my English teacher, either. All I want from you is some clues as to how I can get A's this coming quarter."

Obviously this boy was not in touch with reality, and all I could do was to give him what help I could in English and let him learn that GPA—that great leveler—is no respecter of persons.

"All right, Jerry, the next time I assign a paper, you write it once, and then rewrite it. I think you have been handing me your first draft. From now on, when you have done your second draft, bring it to me ahead of time, and we will go over it."

"Really? Will you help me with each paper, even though you are later going to grade it?"

"Of course, but remember, I don't want to spend time on your first draft. You do your best, and then I will help you with it."

Little did I realize what I was getting into. Jerry brought me his papers each time, and I carefully tutored him. One thing began to impress me—this boy meant business. No effort was too much. Other teachers to whom I talked mentioned that he was camping on their doorsteps, demanding help in making the kind of grades he would need in order to qualify for medicine. Without exception they shared my feeling that, although he was a good boy, he was not a potential doctor.

The following year I had occasion to visit with Jerry from time to time, and always asked how he was doing in his studies. The answer seldom varied—he was getting B's and occasionally A's. I noticed that he never ran for student office and did not turn out for sports. He mentioned one time that his Saturday nights were set aside for reviewing classes that he was worried about. It appeared to me that he did not know there were any girls on campus.

By the time his graduation rolled around, none of us were surprised that he had a good enough GPA to be accepted at Loma Linda. Today he is a practicing physician, and if I were within reach of him, Jerry would be my doctor. He taught me more than I taught him.

One Supreme Court Justice made the statement "I am an example of plodding mediocrity." I know of no tests that can measure motivation adequately. Aptitude, achievement, preferences, interests, and weaknesses are all measurable, but the precious fire of zeal defies qualification. Jerry and his kind will ever baffle the testmakers and prognosticators, and inspire their fellows. Jerry taught me that I should never underestimate the potential of the dedicated student. In the years since he sat in my class, I have often faced students who seemed to have unrealistic plans for the future. As a counselor and as a believer in the power of the Holy Spirit and the will, I am increasingly more reluctant to set limits for young people who have aspirations. Occasionally I point out the difficulties along the way to their goals, but I hope never to be guilty of discouraging one who is inspired to reach the heights.

CONCLUSION

At the outset, I expressed a desire to provide some help and enlightenment for two groups of concerned Christians—those who are contemplating careers as counselors, and those teachers or pastors or youth workers who may currently be doing some counseling, either formally or informally. A friend who read the manuscript remarked that it was just a collection of stories. So be it. Jesus never taught without illustrations, so there is good precedent, and I cannot preach or teach without analogy either. When I need to define an abstraction, I can only do so in concrete terms, and that means using anecdotes. The ultimate example of the unknown being illustrated by the known is found in John 1:14, where we are told that "the Word was made flesh, and dwelt among us."

To me, patience is not a word, but a kind teacher painstakingly drilling me on the conjugation of Spanish verbs, or another practicing scales and arpeggios with me, when I preferred to be outside playing softball. Love is not a four-letter, monosyllabic abstraction, but a wife who knows all about me, including my considerable accumulation of foibles and weaknesses, but who for three and a half decades continues to care and to challenge me to improve.

Motivation is not a catchword in the jargon of the behavioral scientists, but Jerry, the intellectual mediocrity who refused to be intimidated by his limitations, and graduated from medicine. Prodigality is not only the ancient story of the spendthrift son, squandering his inheritance in riotous living, but Tyrone, with his lavish endowments of talent and charm, wasting them and disappointing those who loved him.

So, I do not apologize for telling stories; I know no other way to say what I want to say. And what I want to say is that the world needs sympathetic, caring listeners, counselors who do not scold, who keep confidences, who can hold onto the unpromising, fumbling sinner with one hand while keeping the other firmly in the grasp of the Great Counselor. Since all have sinned and come short of the glory of God, none can pose as good, or holy, or better than his fellow man. Therefore, we must all be humble, before our counselees and before our Lord.

Further, I have tried to convey the message that the giving of advice is not only dangerous but markedly unfruitful. Only when the counselee makes decisions for himself, with such information as he and the counselor can generate, and with the assurance that divine help is always available—only then can he make real progress.

So the counselor is at best merely a catalyst, which by definition is an agent that facilitates a reaction without itself becoming a part of the finished product. Perhaps that analogy is slightly flawed, for in my own experience I have been changed by every interaction with the youth across the desk from me. Unlike the catalyst, which remains unchanged, I have been actively involved. However, the counselee does move on, while the counselor remains behind to share the next student's problems, and the next, and the next.

If the reader has gained some insight from these pages, I will feel gratified. Certainly this small book does not cover the whole topic, nor does it pretend to. No attempt has been made to be scholarly or to discuss the pros and cons of the many good theories that bear the names of the famous writers and practitioners in the field, although I do not wish to belittle the importance of any of the fine writers whose works have been helpful. The two best sources of wisdom to me are the Bible and the Holy Spirit, freely available to all who seek. Other "authorities" become sort of footnotes, good when they echo or reflect the Scriptures, and bad when they deviate from them.